An Introduction
to Professional and
Executive Coaching

A volume in
Contemporary Trends in Organization Development and Change
Peter Sorensen and Therese Yaeger, *Series Editors*

Contemporary Trends in Organization Development and Change

Peter Sorensen and Therese Yaeger, *Series Editors*

An Introduction to Professional and Executive Coaching

Sheila Boysen-Rotelli

Lewis University

INFORMATION AGE PUBLISHING, INC.
Charlotte, NC • www.infoagepub.com

Library of Congress Cataloging-in-Publication Data

A CIP record for this book is available from the Library of Congress
http://www.loc.gov

ISBN: 978-1-64113-254-1 (Paperback)
        978-1-64113-255-8 (Hardcover)
        978-1-64113-256-5 (ebook)

*To my parents who started me down the path of knowledge,
to Graham, who has unwaveringly traveled this path with me,
and to my Finn and Blaney who continuously open my eyes
to new adventures along the way.*

Contents

Foreword

We are proud to present a new addition to our Contemporary Trends in Organization Development and Change book series with this book on Coaching by Sheila M. Boysen-Rotelli, PhD. The inclusion of her book in this series reflects the evolution of coaching as a major intervention in the field of organization development (OD). This evolution is illustrated by, for example, the fact that in the early introductory textbooks in the field by Cummings and Huse (1975) there was no mention of coaching. In another early textbook (French and Bell, 1978), if one looks for the term coaching the reader is referred to the concept of mentoring.

The current status of coaching in OD is reflected in an entire chapter devoted to the subject by Burke and Noumair in "Organization Development: A Process of Learning and Changing" (2015). An even stronger illustration of the role of coaching in OD today is the Shull, Church, and Burke (2013) article reporting their results of a major survey of OD professionals in which they report that coaching is seen as an integral part of OD, as one of five major themes reported for the field. In their comments on coaching and OD, the authors state, the growth of coaching as a core OD activity is not all that surprising given the traditional value of the humanistic approach in the field.

Dr. Boysen-Rotelli provides us with a comprehensive introduction to the field, an introduction which provides meaningful material for both the scholar and the practitioner. In Dr. Boysen-Rotelli's writing, she also shares

An Introduction to Professional and Executive Coaching, pages xi–xii
Copyright © 2018 by Information Age Publishing
xi

her work and insights to coaching based on her own work as both a scholar and a practitioner.

Again, we welcome Dr. Boysen-Rotelli to our book series with a critical book on what has become a major intervention in our field.

—**Peter F. Sorensen, PhD**
Therese F. Yaeger, PhD

References

Burke, W., & Noumair, D. (2015). *Organization development: A process of learning and changing* (3rd ed.). Indianapolis, IN: Pearson FT Press.

Cummings, T. G., & Huse, E. F. (1975). *Organization development and change.* St. Paul, MN: West.

French, W. L., & Bell, C. (1978). *Organization development.* Englewood Cliffs, NJ: Prentice Hall.

Shull, A., Church, A., & Burke, W. (2013). Attitudes about the field of organization development 20 years later: the more things change, the more they stay the same. *Research in Organizational Change and Development, 21,* 1–28.

Preface

The coaching profession is growing. According to the International Coach Federation (ICF), coaching earns over $2 billion per year in U.S. dollars. This book serves as a resource for both practitioners and scholars of professional coaching.

The ICF conducts a global study every 4 years. Their most recent study found that there are over 54,000 practitioners of coaching across the world. It also found that almost all coach practitioners received some form of coach specific training and development. This book is for the developing coach practitioner as well as the experienced coach practitioner that would like to develop further. Coaching is an exciting and powerful skill set that allows practitioners to empower others and helps individuals to generate awareness that opens the door for great levels of success.

The approach of this book is to look at the theoretical framework of coaching as it applies to the actual practice of coaching others and groups. The foundation of this book is based on the ICF's 11 core competencies of coaching, the most widely accepted coaching principles in the industry and profession of coaching. Also discussed is an overview of how to build an independent coaching business.

It is important to ground practice in theory and research to bring together the researched framework to help to inform the approach. There is an old proverb that states: "Theory is when you know everything but nothing works. Practice is when everything works, but no one knows why." The approach of this book will enable the reader with the theory, the processes,

An Introduction to Professional and Executive Coaching, pages xiii–xiv
Copyright © 2018 by Information Age Publishing

and the skills to coach in a way that works, and to be able to understand the why behind the success as well as make it replicable.

It is the author's hope that the readers of this book will find information that is relevant, helpful, and even challenging in ways that increase their personal growth and development as coaches.

1

Coaching Overview and Definition

Welcome to the start of your coaching knowledge journey! True coaching presence is a way of "being" much more so than a way of "doing." For this reason, coaching is a lifelong learning endeavor. Even the most masterful coaches have the opportunity to become more masterful. After reading this book, working through the practice questions and the exercises, you will be ready to coach others. However, the journey of becoming a practitioner of coaching requires practice, reflection, and an ongoing openness to your own personal growth and development.

Coaching is exciting and very rewarding. Coaching can unlock hidden potential that has not been able to be tapped into by any other development avenue. Coaching is a tool that injects awareness into a client's world in a way that can bring about success that they were not able to achieve without coaching. It can be argued that those are some big claims, however, as you set out on your own coaching education and journey of development you will quickly see these results for yourself.

This chapter will introduce and cover the current definitions of coaching as well as explore how coaching compares and contrasts to the other

An Introduction to Professional and Executive Coaching, pages 1–18
Copyright © 2018 by Information Age Publishing

helping interventions such as mentoring, therapy, tutoring, consulting, and athletic coaching. In addition, it will explore each of the International Coach Federation (ICF) 11 core competencies of coaching and how these competencies play a role in effective coaching engagements.

Coaching Defined

Coaching is a process and a profession that has grown dramatically during the past decade. Williams (2007) states, "Coaching is the second-fastest growing profession, rivaled only by information technology" (p. 1). Morgan, Harkins, and Goldsmith (2005) echo this view stating, "Coaching is an exploding industry" (p. 1). They add that "more and more coaches, from an ever-widening circle of backgrounds and schools of thought, offer their services to organizations and individuals" (p. 1). The profession has some coaches that consider themselves generalists, whereas other coaches have niches or specializations including executive coaching, behavioral coaching, career coaching, leadership development coaching, organizational change coaching, strategy coaching, diversity coaching, emotional competence coaching, change and transition coaching, alignment coaching, spiritual coaching, philosophical coaching, and ethics coaching. Executive coaching is the use of coaching within management levels, most commonly inside an organization, but can also be contracted by an individual outside of the organization (Lazar & Bergquist, 2004; Morgan et al., 2005; Ting & Scisco, 2006).

Coaching is a growing phenomenon. However, this growing phenomenon is yet to have a universally recognized definition; instead, countless definitions from many different sources attempt to summarize the concept, process, and profession of coaching. One of the reasons for such a montage of definitions is that some researchers focus on coaching in organizations, some on one-on-one coaching, and some on group coaching. Moreover, many different coaching specializations shape some of the definitions. Nevertheless, some commonalities do exist. Most definitions focus on some type of professional development, change, growth, or thriving. Peterson and Hicks (1996) describe coaching as "the process of equipping people with tools, knowledge, and opportunities they need to develop themselves and become more effective" (p. 14). King and Eaton (1999) describe it as "a structured two-way process which develops and harnesses a person's talents in the pursuit of specific goals" (p. 145). Tobias (1996) says, "The term coaching has the advantage of implying an ongoing process" (p. 116), which, as he points out, distinguishes it from other onetime activities such as workshops and seminars. He adds that coaching is individually tailored to the person and the current issue or problem, as opposed to the "one-size-fits-all" menu that other development interventions present. This idea is supported by Witherspoon and White (1996a) who agree that coaching is a customized, individualized, one-on-one partnership in which there is a recognition that no two people are alike. Each person has a unique knowledge base, learning pace, and learning style.

A few additional definitions include:

The art of facilitating the performance, learning and development of another. (Downey, 2003, p. 21)

Unlocking people's potential to maximize their own performance. It is helping them to learn rather than teaching them. (Whitmore, 2009, p. 11)

A human development process that involved structured, focused interaction and the use of appropriate strategies, tool and techniques to promote desirable and sustainable change for the benefit of the client and potentially for other stakeholders. (Cox, Bachkirova & Clutterbuck, 2010, p. 1)

Many view coaching as a partnership of collaboration. Whitworth, Kimsey-House, and Sandahl (1998), who are associated with the Coaches Training Institute, have specifically characterized their approach to coaching as "Co-Active because it involves the active and collaborative participation of both the coach and the client" (p. xi). In their view, both parties are actively and equally engaged in the coaching partnership, and therefore they have deemed this as co-active. Professional coaches provide an ongoing partnership designed to help clients produce fulfilling results in their personal and professional lives.

Some definitions are more suited for a work or business environment because they include the relationship among the individual client, the coach, and the employer. Linkage (as cited in Goldsmith, Lyons, & Freas, 2000) says, "The best coaching occurs within context, working with individual leaders to drive personal behavioral change against the backdrop of the business strategy and the larger team" (p. xvii). Furthermore, Linkage argues that coaching must be grounded in the practical and geared toward action. In other words, the coaching must generate results not just for the client but also for the client's company. The concept that coaching is a long-term process that benefits both the person and the organization in which that person works is a definition held by Goldsmith et al. (2000). Specifically, they see coaching as a behavioral approach of mutual benefit to individuals and the organizations in which they work or network. It is not merely a technique or onetime event; it is a strategic process that adds value both to the people being coached and to the bottom line of the organization.

ICF, which is the most recognized governing and credentialing body of the coaching profession, defines coaching as: "Partnering with clients in a thought-provoking and creative process that inspires the client to maximize their personal and professional potential in today's uncertain and complex environments. Coaches honor the client as the expert in his or her life and work and believe every client is creative, resourceful and whole." (ICF, 2017, para. 5).

The cornerstones of coaching are:

- The client is naturally creative, resourceful, and whole.
- Coaching addresses the whole person.
- The agenda comes from the client and not from the coach.
- The coach and client partner and work together as equals; based on mutual respect.
- Coaching is about action that inspires change.

At the most basic level, the coach's responsibility is to

- discover, clarify, and align with what the client wants to achieve;
- encourage client's self-discovery;
- elicit client-generated solutions and strategies; and
- Hold the client responsible and accountable.

Based on these definitions in the literature, the following definition is used in this book: *Effective coaching is a transformational process where the coach is the catalyst and the client gains awareness around solutions, answers, and shifts that will help them to achieve goals and reach a state of thriving.* Specifically, the term "thriving" is used because of its relevance in the literature review and the implied sustainability that accompanies the term.

How Coaching Is Different

The foundations of the coaching process promote inquiry, challenging thinking patterns, and creates new ways of thinking, being, and acting. Every coaching conversation is based on the client's agenda and requires a partnership of equals while assuming the client is whole and not broken in any way.

Because of the various definitions of coaching, it is important to call out the differences with other seemingly similar terms. Here is a brief description of these other terms to show that they are, in fact, different from coaching:

Mentoring

Distinct differences exist between coaching and mentoring. Ting and Scisco (2006) describe a mentor as "someone who has a certain set of knowledge and skills that are passed on to others" (p. 72). The ICF (2017) views mentoring as "guiding another person based upon one's own experience" (para. 3). Often, the mentor is more experienced than their mentee and seen as wiser than the mentee. Elements of advice, guiding, and training are part of most mentoring relationships. Coaching may be used as part of a mentoring engagement, but the role of the mentor extends outside of the coaching process. In the coaching relationship, the coach and the coachee are equals and work together to help the client direct and explore his or her own learning.

Therapy

Coaching also differs from therapy. For example, Grant (2007) reports that the "key foci in coaching is striving for and attaining goals, along with enhancing one's well-being, whereas in therapy the key foci is on the treatment of psychopathology" (p. 61). Grant points out that only limited empirical research has explored the boundaries between coaching and therapy. When specifically considering executives, one difference between coaching and therapy is that executive coaching tends to be focused on an issue such as job performance and interpersonal skills. It also occurs in the workplace and is intended to improve the executive's performance, (Kampa-Kokesch & Anderson, 2010). The settings in which coaching may take place are vast, including in-person, meetings with the client's colleagues, observation sessions, and communications via telephone or e-mail. On the other hand, therapy occurs mostly in the counselor's office (Rotenberg, 2000). Moreover, the length of a coaching session can vary dramatically, whereas a therapy session is often a set amount of time in length (Kampa-Kokesch & Anderson, 2010).

The confusion between coaching and therapy may be due to the disciplines that both professions draw from a theoretical framework perspective. Examples would be solution-focused theory, cognitive theory and neuro linguistic programming ([NLP], all discussed in Chapter 3). In recent years, many clinical therapists have reinvented themselves as coaching professionals. The distinction between therapy and coaching tends to be the most confusing to the general public. Unlike the history of coaching, the history of therapy spans more than a century. The American Psychological Association (2016) defines psychotherapy as "a partnership between an individual

TABLE 1.1 Therapy and Coaching Distinctions	
Therapy	**Coaching**
Assumes the client needs healing.	Assumes the client is whole.
Roots in medicine, psychiatry.	Root in sports and business
Works with people to achieve self-understanding and emotional healing.	Works to move people to a higher level of functioning.
Focuses on feeling and event.	Focuses and action and the future.
Explores the root of the problem.	Focuses on solving problems.
Works to bring the unconscious into the consciousness.	Works with the conscious mind.
Works for internal resolution of pain and to let go of old patterns.	Works for external solutions to overcome barriers, learn new skills and implement effective choices.

and a professional such as a psychologist who is licensed and trained to help people understand their feelings and assist with changing their behavior" (p. 52). Table 1.1 gives an overview of some of the main distinctions to delineate therapy and coaching.

Tutoring and Training

Typically, in training or tutoring, the aim is to impart or help someone gain a specific new knowledge or skill set (Kinlaw, 2000). This includes improving specific technical competencies and understanding, and becoming knowledgeable in a specific discipline. A central difference between training and coaching is that a trainer defines the learning outcome or the standard to be achieved where the process in coaching is negotiated between the coach and client.

Consulting

Consulting occurs when an organization retains another party for the purpose of accessing specialized expertise to diagnose and, at times, implement solutions. The difference with coaching is that the client is viewed as being capable of generating his or her own solutions, with the coach acting in a role that prompts self-discovery. The coach views the client with a positive regard, capable of uncovering answers to his or her problems rather than a person that needs to be fixed (Passmore, 2007). The main difference between a consultant and a coach is that the main process of a consultant involves telling based on expertise and the main process of a coach involves asking based on the coaching process.

Managing and Supervising

Managing and supervising are two terms that have many different meanings and nuances. In the broadest context, a manager or supervisor is someone who oversees work and they are very advisory in their role. This is distinctly different from coaching in that a coach does not advise and is not responsible for the client's performance or the oversight of their work.

Athletic Coaching

Although sports metaphors are often used in coaching, professional coaching is different from the traditional sports coaching. Athletic coaching may be one of the first things that comes to mind for people when talking about coaching. Athletic coaches are often seen as experts who guide and direct the behavior of individuals or teams based on their greater experience and knowledge. Professional coaches possess these qualities, but it is the experience as well as the knowledge of the individual or team that determines the direction. Additionally, professional coaching, unlike athletic development, does not focus on behaviors that are being executed poorly or incorrectly. Instead, the focus is on identifying opportunity for development based on individual strengths and capabilities (Passmore, 2007; Whitworth et al., 1998).

Example

Let's take a look at a simplistic example that helps to differentiate between coaching and other helping professions and interventions: *riding a bike.*

The *counselor* would help you discover what is holding you back from riding the bike. They would go back into your past to discover what kind of experience you had at an early age with a bicycle.

The *consultant* would bring you a bicycle manual and tell you everything you ever wanted to know about the workings of a bicycle. The consultant would then depart and return 6 months later to see how you were doing.

The *mentor* would share their experiences of bike riding and the lessons they learned. The mentor would bestow all the wisdom they had about bicycle riding to you.

The *coach* would help you get on the bicycle and then encourage, endorse, acknowledge, and support you while running alongside until you felt comfortable enough to do it alone.

Coaching Organizations and Governing Bodies

There are a number of coaching organizations across the world. These organizations include: the Association of Coach Training Organizations, Association for Coaching, The British Psychological Society's Special Group in Coaching Psychology, European Mentoring and Coaching Council, International Associate of Coaching, Graduate School Alliance of Executive Coaching, International Association of Coaching, and Standards Australia. Each of these organizations adds great value to the field and profession of coaching. However, the ICF is considered to be the "gold standard" of the field of coaching with organizations such as the International Association of Coaching (IAC) being recognized as a secondary but also well-respected credential provider.

The ICF is a nonprofit organization dedicated to professional coaching. Currently, the ICF has approximately 30,000 members in 140 countries. Founded in 1995, the ICF campaigns worldwide for professional standards within the coaching profession, and provides independent certification for professional coaches (through their credential process) and coach training programs (through their approval and accreditation process). The ICF has become recognized as the main accrediting and credentialing body for both training programs and coaches across the world. The ICF has made great efforts to standardize and professionalize the field of coaching.

TABLE 1.2   ICF 11 Core Competencies
A. Setting the Foundation
1. Meeting Ethical Guidelines and Professional Standards
2. Establishing the Coaching Agreement
B. Co-Creating the Relationship
3. Establishing Trust and Intimacy with the Client
4. Coaching Presence
C. Communicating Effectively
5. Active Listening
6. Powerful Questioning
7. Direct Communication
D. Facilitating Learning and Results
8. Creating Awareness
9. Designing Actions
10. Planning and Goal Setting
11. Managing Progress and Accountability

As part of those efforts, the ICF has created a list of 11 core competencies that coaches should embody (Table 1.2). They include four categories: setting the foundation, co-creating the relationship, communicating effectively, and facilitating learning and results. The ICF has undergone the process of formalizing these competencies even further by developing a list of professional certified coach (PCC) markers that specify coaching behavior for more consistent and objective assessment of coaching mastery. These markers for behavioral assessment as well as specific examples of what they look like in a coaching engagement can be found in the appendix of this book. Next, we will discuss each of these 11 competencies.

International Coach Federation 11 Core Competencies

1. Meeting Ethical Guidelines and Professional Standards

This competency is the ability to apply coaching ethics and standards in all coaching situations. This competency is exhibited when the coach

- understands and exhibits in own behaviors the ICF standards of conduct;
- understands and follows all ICF ethical guidelines;
- clearly communicates the distinctions between coaching, consulting, psychotherapy, and other support professions; and
- refers client to another support professional as needed, knowing when this is needed and the available resources.

2. Establishing the Coaching Agreement

This competency is defined as the ability to understand what is required in the specific coaching interaction and to come to an agreement with the prospective and new client about the coaching process and relationship. Coaches must know what is required in the coaching interaction and be in agreement with the client about the coaching process and relationship. Some example questions that help to showcase this competency are:

- What outcomes do you want to see as a result of the coaching?
- How will you know we have been successful?
- What will be different if we reach that outcome today?

3. Establishing Trust and Intimacy With the Client

This competency is about creating a safe, supportive environment that produces ongoing mutual respect and trust. The client will experience trust and intimacy when the coach believes completely that the client is a being of brilliance with unlimited potential. Also, clients experience trust and intimacy when they can share their hopes, dreams, disappointments, and frustrations, without fear of being judged or exposed at some later point in the relationship.

Coaches can create trust by

- believing wholly that each and every client is brilliant, has the answers needed to live their highest and best good, and can conquer areas of life that have not been fulfilled;
- walking in humble confidence (demonstrating masterful coaching skills without requiring praise or recognition from the client; It's about them, not you!);
- acting selflessly (keeping the conversation focused on the client, sharing personal information only as it supports the client's ongoing development, and facilitating the conversation with the client's higher agenda in mind);
- ensuring confidentiality (mentioning this in pre-coaching written agreements as well as verbalizing this at the beginning of the coaching); and
- being consistently professional and trustworthy (the client can count on you to do what you say you will do; any negative emotions are kept in check even when you're experiencing stress).

4. Coaching Presence

Coaching presence is defined as the ability to be fully conscious and create a spontaneous relationship with the client, employing a style that is open, flexible and confident. Coaching presence can be exemplified when the coach

- is present and flexible during the coaching process, dancing in the moment;
- accesses their own intuition and trusts their inner knowing (i.e., "goes with their gut");
- is open to not knowing and takes risks in the coaching conversation;

- sees many ways to work with the client, and chooses in the moment what is most effective;
- uses humor effectively to create lightness and energy;
- confidently shifts perspectives and experiments with new possibilities for own action; and
- demonstrates confidence in working with strong emotions, and can self-manage and not be overpowered or enmeshed by client's emotions.

5. Active Listening

Active Listening is listening not just for the client's words, but for what is not being spoken, as well as the energy/emotion behind the words. It involves responding in a manner that allows the client to articulate what is true and uplifting for him or her. The coach focuses completely on what the client is and is not saying, attends to the client and client's agenda and not to the coach's agenda for the client, and understands the meaning of what is said in the context of the client's desires. When you are operating in a mode of active listening, you are supporting and encouraging the client's self-expression and distinguishing between the words, the tone of voice, and the body language. Some tools that showcase active listening are

- summarizing, paraphrasing, and mirroring back what the client has said to ensure clarity and understanding;
- integrating and building on client's ideas and suggestions;
- "bottom-lining" or understanding the essence of the client's communication; and
- allowing the client to vent or "clear" the situation without judgment or attachment in order to move on to next steps.

6. Powerful Questions

Powerful questioning requires asking questions that reflect active listening and an understanding of the client's perspective. It includes questions that evoke discovery, insight, commitment, or action. The most powerful questions are open-ended questions that create greater clarity and the possibility for new learning. Power comes from questions that move the client toward what they desire, not questions that ask for the client to justify or look backward. Coaches should focus on questions that uncover information that serves the client and the coaching relationship by using "what" questions. "What" questions lead the client to an ideal state, while "how" questions are strategy questions (how will this be accomplished?). In the powerful questioning process, it can help to hold these "how" questions until the "what" is clarified. Some example questions that help to showcase this competency follow:

- What's the question that needs to be answered?
- What else?
- What's the truth about that? What would your closest friend/biggest fan say is true?
- If your colleagues or manager were to give you anonymous feedback that was completely candid, what might they say about that? What might be hard to hear?
- There are a number of "I can'ts" in that description. What would it look like if you could? Who would you need to become to make that happen?
- What values do you want to honor as you consider this decision?
- As you think about the legacy you want to leave, how will that influence your actions?
- What do you know about yourself that will enable you to manage this challenge?

7. Direct Communication

Direct communication means communicating effectively during coaching sessions and using language that has a positive impact on the client. It is about being clear, articulate, and direct in sharing and providing feedback. It involves reframing to help the client understand another perspective that he/she wants or is uncertain about. Direct communication involves clearly stating the coaching objectives, meeting agenda, and purpose of techniques or exercises that are used during coaching. Some example questions that help to showcase this competency follows:

- I truly hear your concern, a question is coming to mind and I'd like to ask it in support of you, "How might this problem be perfect?"
- If the client seems confused by the question, ask, "Does the question make sense?" In other words, "What have you learned about yourself that will allow you to manage this successfully?"
- What's important to focus on today?
- What would you like coaching on?
- What's on your mind today?

8. Creating Awareness

Creating awareness involves integrating and evaluating information that helps the client gain awareness and achieve agreed upon results. The simple fact is that words are powerful. Our words have the capacity to either empower or disable clients. Ask yourself, does this question/comment allow the client to be in a place of peace and possibility, or does it cause a "fight-flight-or-freeze" defensive response? For example, instead of saying, "that's been a problem area for you in the past," consider saying, "that's a 'calling forth' area that you've been focusing on and making progress in." Some example questions that help to showcase this competency are:

- How would you connect the dots in all of this?
- What would allow you to keep your antennae up around this situation?
- As you approach this situation/person, what do you want to be aware of?
- How do your beliefs/actions impact people/situations?
- What awareness do you have about how others perceive this/you?
- What choices do you have the power to make?

9. Designing Actions

Designing actions is the coach's ability to partner with their client to create opportunities for ongoing learning, during coaching and in work/life situations, and for taking new actions that will most effectively lead to agreed-upon coaching results. The coach actively works to cocreate opportunities with the client to develop action steps that move them towards their goals and will lead to agreed-upon coaching results. Some example questions that help to showcase this competency are:

- What do you want to teach yourself?
- What structures or systems allow you to learn best?
- What's the root-level learning associated with this?
- What have you learned or relearned about yourself that will keep you in a place of choice? What action would allow you to deepen your learning on this?

10. Planning and Goal Setting

This competency serves to develop and maintain an effective coaching plan with the client. Without plans and goals, there is no coaching. It is unanchored chit-chat. With plans and goals, there can be deliberate, intentional dialogue that leads to a purposeful coaching conversation. Some example questions that help to showcase this competency are:

- What's your plan for making that happen?
- What thoughts do you have for taking action?
- What are some other resources you might tap into for that?
- Who else would be helpful to speak with about that?
- How could you find a research maven to help with that?

11. Managing Progress and Accountability

Managing progress and accountability is all about keeping intention and attention on what is truly important to the client and leaving the responsibility to take action with the client. As a coach, it is important to stay away from giving (consulting/advising) solutions or action steps. Instead, we want to help the client unlock their own ideas for action and how they can be accountable. Some example questions that help to showcase this competency are:

- What do you need, if anything, in order to complete that?
- What else do you need to do?
- What are some possible barriers to taking action?

The IAC has also created a set of coaching standards that they call the coaching masteries:

1. establishing and maintaining a relationship of trust,
2. perceiving affirming and expanding the client's potential,
3. engaged listening,
4. processing in the present,
5. expressing,
6. clarifying,
7. helping the client set and keep clear intentions,
8. inviting possibility, and
9. helping the client create and use supportive systems and structures.

Although they are different in number and in title, there is alignment between these two sets of standards as depicted in Table 1.3. The ICF and the IAC have both contributed to moving coaching towards becoming more professionalized through their standardization and credentialing formalization. Today, based on these criteria, coaching can be considered a profession.

TABLE 1.3 ICF Core Competencies Versus IAC Coaching Masteries

ICF Core Competencies	IAC Coaching Masteries
Meeting Ethical Guidelines and Professional Standards	
Establishing the Coaching Agreement	Establishing and Maintaining a Relationship of Trust
Establishing Trust and Intimacy with the Client	
Coaching Presence	
Active Listening	Engaged Listening
Powerful Questioning	
Direct Communication	Processing in the Present Expressing Clarifying
Creating Awareness	Perceiving, Affirming and Expanding the Client's Potential
Designing Actions	Inviting Possibility
Planning and Goal Setting	Heling the Client Set and Keep Clear Intentions
Managing Progress and Accountability	Helping the Client Create and Use Supporting Systems and Structures

The Profession of Coaching

As the reach and popularity of coaching has increased, there have been a number of organizations, professional bodies, and training programs that have emerged over recent decades. However, there are criteria that need to be met for a discipline to be accepted as a profession.

Bennett (2006) has reviewed the relevant literature and summarized the criteria to enable coaching to be determined a profession as follows:

1. identifiable and distinct skills (i.e., skills that are widely accepted as required for the performance of skilled coaching),
2. education and training required to acquire proficiency (e.g., the minimum initial and ongoing training required to coach, generally accepted competences required for coaches, means of assessing competence),
3. recognition outside the community as a profession (e.g., recognition by established professions as a profession, government classification of coaching as a profession),

4. code of ethics (i.e., a code of ethics for coaches defined, implemented, monitored, and effectively enforced by a governing body; making coaching a self-disciplined industry),
5. public service (public service by coaches that is motivated by altruism rather than financial gain),
6. formalized organization (i.e., widely accepted and established professional association(s) representing the profession and those practicing coaching),
7. evaluation of merit (credentialing) and self-regulation of service (e.g., definition of accepted requirements for coaches, systems for assessing competence, systems for monitoring and regulating service delivery by coaches, mechanisms for encouraging thought and discussion about the practice of coaching),
8. established community of practitioners (e.g., forums where coaches can network and exchange ideas on coaching, publications supporting the community of practitioners),
9. status of membership in a profession (e.g., recognition of coaches by their clients and the general public as members of a profession),
10. public recognition (i.e., recognition by the general public that coaching is a distinct and established profession), and
11. knowledge base (i.e., coaching practice founded in theoretical and factual research and knowledge, with a defined body of knowledge, a defined theoretical foundation, and ongoing evidence-based theoretical and practical research).

Thanks to organizations such as the ICF, the majority of these criteria are being met by the coaching field. For this reason, although in its infancy, coaching can be considered a blooming profession.

Chapter Summary

Coaching has become more and more commonly used, however, there remains a need for additional empirical research on the topic. Although there is somewhat limited empirical research on coaching compared to other professions, the research is mounting and the results are consistently showing evidence that coaching is a powerful and effective tool for professional growth and organizational development.

McDermott, Levinson, and Newton (2007) have stated companies report that coaching has the biggest positive impact on micro-level outcomes such as developing future leaders and improving leadership behaviors and individual employee performance. Moreover, Witherspoon and White (1996b) assert that coaching leads to several positive outcomes, including better decisions, increased options, and enhanced self-awareness. The ICF and the 11 core coaching competencies have catapulted coaching into the realm of a profession and have helped to generate a better understanding of what coaching is as well as the value that coaching provides.

Chapter Reflection Questions

1. How does coaching differ from other service professions?
2. How do the coaching core competencies help to distinguish it from other service professions? Be specific and provide examples.
3. How does the professionalization of coaching benefit coaches and coaching clients?

Activities

1. Write out your talking points on how you will answer the question from others: "What exactly is coaching?" How will you explain it in a clear and compelling way?
2. As you review Bennett's criteria for a field to be considered a profession, where are some of the biggest opportunities in the realm of coaching? How can the profession best strengthen itself?

References

American Psychological Association. (2016). *How to find help through psychotherapy*. Retrieved from http://www.apa.org/helpcenter/therapy.aspx

Bennett, J. L. (2006). An agenda for coaching related research: A challenge for researchers. *Coaching Psychology Journal: Practice and Research, 58*(4), 240–249.

Cox, E., Bachkirova, T., & Clutterbuck, D. (Eds.). (2010). *The complete handbook of coaching*. London, England: SAGE.

Downey, M. (2003). *Effective coaching: Lessons from the coach's coach* (2nd ed.). London, England: Texere.

Goldsmith, M., Lyons, L., & Freas, A. (Eds.). (2000). *Coaching for leadership: How the world's greatest coaches help leaders learn*. San Francisco, CA: John Wiley and Sons.

Grant, A. M. (2007). A languishing-flourishing model of goal striving and mental health for coaching populations. *International Coaching Psychology Review, 2*(3), 250–264.

International Coach Federation. (2017). *How is coaching distinct from other service professions?* Retrieved June 25, 2017 from https://coachfederation.org/faqs

Kampa-Kokesch, S., & Anderson, M. Z. (2010). Executive coaching: A comprehensive review of literature. *Consulting Psychology Journal: Practice and Research, 53*(4), 205–228.

King, P., & Eaton, J. (1999). Coaching for results. *Industrial and Commercial Training, 31*(4), 145–148.

Kinlaw, D. C. (2000). Encourage superior performance from people and teams through coaching. *Women in Business, 52*(1), 38–41.

Lazar, J., & Bergquist, W. (2004). Alignment coaching: A broader perspective on business coaching. *Performance Improvement, 43*(10), 16–22.

McDermott, M., Levenson, A., & Newton, S. (2007). What coaching can and cannot do for your organization. *Human Resource Planning, 30*(2), 30–37.

Morgan, H., Harkins, P., & Goldsmith, M. (Eds.). (2005). *The art and practice of leadership coaching: 50 top executive coaches reveal their secrets.* Hoboken, NJ: Wiley and Sons.

Passmore, J. (2007). An integrative model for executive coaching. *Consulting Psychology Journal: Practice and Research, 59*(1), 68–78.

Peterson, D. B., & Hicks, M. D. (1996). *Leader as coach: Strategies for coaching and developing others.* Minneapolis, MN: Personnel Decisions International.

Rotenberg, C. T. (2000). Psychodynamic psychotherapy and executive coaching: Overlapping paradigms. *Journal of the American Academy of Psychoanalysis, 28*, 653–663.

Ting, S., & Scisco, P. (2006). *The CCL handbook of coaching: A guide for the leader coach.* San Francisco, CA: Jossey-Bass.

Tobias, L. L. (1996). Coaching executives. *Consulting Psychology Journal: Practice and Research, 48*(2), 87–95.

Williams, R. (2007). *The second-fastest growing profession.* Retrieved from http://www.coachfederation.org/ICF/For+Current+Members/Member+Resources/Research/Articles.htm 245

Witherspoon, R., & White, R. P. (1996a). Executive coaching: A continuum of roles. *Consulting Psychology Journal: Practice and Research, 48*(2), 124–133.

Witherspoon, R., & White, R. P. (1996b). Executive coaching: What's in it for you? *Training and Development, 50*(3), 14–16.

Whitmore, J. (2009) *Coaching for Performance: GROWing Human Potential and Purpose: The Principles and Practice of Coaching and Leadership* (4th ed.). London, England: Nicholas Brealey.

Whitworth, L., Kimsey-House, H., & Sandahl, P. (1998). *Co-active coaching: New skills for coaching people toward success in work and life.* Palo Alto, CA: Davies-Black.

2

The Evolution of Coaching

"**P**ut me in coach, I'm ready to play!" As discussed in Chapter 1, many people think of sports coaching when they think of coaching, and for good reason. Coaching has its roots in the area of sports, dating back to ancient Greece.

So, some might argue that workplace coaching goes back centuries to the times of apprenticeships and the most basic and original mentoring relationships. However, the earliest forms of formal coaching as evidenced through the literature comes from the field of business.

This chapter will look at the research that exists around how coaching has developed over the years and decades. It will also examine studies that have been conducted that illuminate the types of outcomes that can be achieved through coaching.

The History of Executive Coaching

Let us look at the term "executive coaching." Just as there is no universal or definitive definition for coaching, neither is there one for executive

An Introduction to Professional and Executive Coaching, pages 19–35
Copyright © 2018 by Information Age Publishing

coaching, although attempts have been made. Kilburg (1996) conducted a literature review on coaching and offers this definition of executive coaching:

> A helping relationship formed between a client who has managerial authority and responsibility in an organization and a consultant [coach] who uses a wide variety of behavioral techniques and methods to help the client achieve a mutually identified set of goals to improve his or her professional performance and personal satisfaction and, consequently, to improve the effectiveness of the client's organization within a formally defined coaching agreement. (p. 142)

McDermott, Levenson, and Newton (2007) see executive coaching as "one-on-one interventions with an individual who is not the executive's supervisor, where the focus is on job-related issues such as demonstrating leadership behaviors, new job transitions, and job performance/avoiding derailment" (p. 31). They further contend that the focus is on helping professionals or executives navigate through such issues by making their own decisions rather than the coach directing the specific actions to take.

Although the exact history of executive coaching is not certain, it does have some framework that is believed to have started as early as the 1950s. Through the work of Harris (1999), three phases of the development of coaching have been acknowledged.

The first occurred between 1950 and 1979 when a small number of professionals employed a blend of psychological and organizational development (OD) approaches when working with executives. Then, according to Harris (1999), from 1980 to 1994, there was an increase in the profession and some standardizations started to fall into place. Finally, the third phase, from 1995 to present, has seen a rise in the number of publications on the subject of coaching, along with the establishment of the International Coach Federation (ICF), which is the governing body of the profession (originally called the Professional and Personal Coaches Association).

The profession of executive coaching as we know it today, can specifically be traced back the 1980s. Tobias (1996) claims that the term first entered the business world vocabulary during this decade. He further suggests that one of the reasons that the term "coaching" was first utilized is because the expression "coaching" is less threatening and more readily accepted than terms such as consulting or counseling; thus, it was readily accepted in the turbulent business environment of the time.

It was a time of large scale downsizing in the corporate arena that led to the upheaval of internal training and mentoring programs that had previously enabled and facilitated the career path of successful executives. With the slashing of organizational budgets came the end of executive education and development assistance in the form of internal training and education. This created a new environment and culture that did not offer the same level of in-house developmental support to the management and leadership levels of organizations as previously offered. At this point, some very observant and opportunistic consultants embraced the opportunity to add "executive coaching" to their service offerings.

During this decade, a handful of coaching schools started popping up on the horizon and recruiting coaching students. Another result of this downturn of the economy in the 1980s was a large population of well-educated and displaced executives or unfulfilled high-level professionals that enrolled in coach training in the hopes of a greater degree of career autonomy and a more meaningful career opportunity. These first few coaching schools were all private, for-profit organizations that were forced to invent curriculum as they went, which created a flurry of untested, and in many cases, lack luster quality coach training programs.

Over time, it became apparent that if coaching was going to become more professionalized and fully recognized as a field of merit and a profession, it would need standardization.

The ICF was formed in the mid 1990s to standardize coaching, certify new coaches and accredit coaching training programs. The ICF was able to tame some of the "wild west" behavior that threatened the coaching profession and its credibility. Eventually, the most widely accepted coaching standards were created with the 11 core coaching competencies and rigorous criteria were created to evaluate, approve, and accredit training programs. Along with these enhancements, the ICF created an equally rigorous certification process that demands many years of documented experience, training, and proven competency.

According to Judge and Cowell (1997), executive coaching became more utilized and evident in organizations and practice by the 1990s. Axmith (2004) agrees, stating that executive coaching is a relatively new area of management consulting that has emerged primarily because of the increased pressure on senior executives and believes it will continue to grow into the awareness of the business sector and general public. Since the 1990s, this relatively new area of management development has grown very rapidly. The number of executive coaches in the United States has been estimated in the tens of thousands and continues to increase. Today, more and more organizations are embracing coaching as a powerful development tool for their employees.

The Disciplines That Contribute to Coaching

Although coaching is in its infancy compared to most of the fields and disciplines that underpin it, it is becoming increasingly popular and has benefited organizations across all industries and cultures. Coaching has roots in a number of different fields and bodies of knowledge. Table 2.1 gives an overview of

TABLE 2.1 Fields and Disciplines Which Underpin Coaching	
1. Ontology, epistemology, and phenomenology	Theories drawn from philosophy, philosophy of science, cultural and physical anthropology, and sociology of knowledge. What makes us human? To what extent are we genetically determined? How do we know what we know? What do we take as evidence? Is mere knowledge enough? What's important to us? Is there such a thing as free will?
2. Individual differences and development	Theories drawn from developmental psychology, psychiatry, cognitive psychology, and neuroscience. Who am I? How did I get to be that way? Am I still changing? Does anyone else think like I do? Am I the only one? Am I normal?
3. Motivation, emotion, and behavior	Theories drawn from affective psychology, physiology, psychoanalysis, psychotherapy, personality and social psychology. Why do I feel the way I do? Why do I do what I do? Where do feelings come from? How do I know if my feelings are true? How can I influence others?
4. Thinking, learning, and insight	Theories drawn from cognitive psychology, cognitive science, adult learning studies, and social-cognitive-affective neuroscience. How do I find out what I need to know? What conditions help me learn it? How do I remember it? Why do I remember some things and not others? Why was it so much easier to learn when I was a child? If a memory is really vivid, is it true? How do I remember things in the future? How can I find things I know that I know but can't remember? How can I make an "aha" more likely?
5. Theories of health and wellness	Theories drawn from research on expertise and mastery, creativity, physiology, medicine, mindfulness studies, and sport psychology. How can I get and stay healthy? What should everyone know about how our bodies work? What is health beyond absence of disease? How do I reach for and sustain optimum performance? How does stress affect my health? What does mindfulness have to do with being well? How do our physical brains and bodies, our thinking processes, and our social connections relate to being truly healthy?
6. Interpersonal dynamics and communication	Theories drawn from attachment research, communications studies, neuropsychiatry, comparative neuroscience, family therapy, women's studies, and leadership studies. How can we get along? Why do relationships seem so important? What does it mean to really connect with someone else? How can we stop fighting so much? Is it more important to connect or to be right? What kind of relationship serves coaching best? What does it mean

(continued)

TABLE 2.1 Fields and Disciplines Which Underpin Coaching (cont.)	
	to have a collaborative, contingent conversation? What triggers threat reactions? What happens to my thinking ability when I am stressed? How can I calm feelings of threat?
7. Individual change management	Theories drawn from psychotherapy, positive psychology, narrative and metaphor studies, and brain science. Why is change so hard? Why is it so easy to change in ways I don't want? What role does practice play in change? What role does attention play? What about imagination? What changes when I start doing something different? Can I just get rid of old habits? Can an old dog learn new tricks? How is coaching like self-directed neuroplasticity? What is better for getting myself to change—the carrot or the stick?
8. Group and inter-group dynamics	Theories drawn from social psychology, sociology, anthropology, counseling, diversity studies, conflict and alternate dispute resolution, and economic and political theory. Who is "we" and who is "them" and what difference does that make? What's the effect of being in an out-group? What will make a group like or at least tolerate members of another group? How can we get rid of stereotypes, prejudice, and discrimination? How can we reduce conflict and encourage reconciliation and forgiveness? Is conflict between groups automatic and unchangeable? What are the advantages of diversity? How can we take advantage of the advantages?
9. Social systems and dynamics	Theories drawn from general systems, family systems, social psychology, social networks, sociology, mathematics, biology, cosmology, and climatology. What is a system? How does it change? How does a system achieve dynamic stability? What patterns emerge from chaos? What are the characteristics of complex systems?
10. Organizational systems and dynamics	Theories drawn from action research, leadership, appreciative and positive organizational scholarship, industrial/organizational psychology, management science, human relations, and human capital movement. How do we get organized? What is leadership? How do leaders lead? How do we get things done? How do we coordinate and collaborate? How can we get an organization to act in concert, toward a common goal? What are the characteristics of a healthy organization?
11. Coaching theory and principles	Theories drawn from coaching, coaching research, human relations studies, management education, organizational development, project management, and other precursors to coaching. What are the theoretical foundations of individual and organizational coaching? What promotes cohesion and integration of the field? What are the personal skills, knowledge, and attitudes required of a coach in general and an executive/organizational coach in particular?
12. Organizational change	Theories drawn from organizational development and design, management science, human resources theory, and change management theory. How do organizations grow, develop, flourish, wane, and exit?

Source: GSAEC Academic Standard #7: Theory and Knowledge

the various disciplines that have informed and shaped the field of coaching. As you can see, coaching truly is a multidisciplinary field that draws on some of the most important helping and development fields in existence.

Historical Evidence of Coaching in Organizations

The profession of coaching belongs in the field of OD as an important intervention process and leadership development tool. The power of coaching comes from the practice of powerful questioning to help the clients and the organization realize a level of success that they would not be able to reach on their own.

The historical literature describing the origins of interventions and the experience of the founding contributors to the field of OD includes many aspects of coaching. This evidence of coaching is scattered in discussions of the consultant's interaction with clients as well as in various documented intervention processes and models. This initially scattered material is what became the field of coaching. In his book *Productive Workplaces Revisited*, Weisbord (2004) presents the scenario of a business professional who serves as a coach to workers and a manager in the Calico Mills in India by utilizing his expertise as a catalyst for change.

Weisbord (2004) also shares a story about his friend Don Kirchhoffer who served as both Weisbord's coach and personal consultant. As a consultant, Kirchhoffer taught new ideas, offered advice of how to implement those ideas, and suggested books, all of which stimulated new thinking for Weisbord. Enthusiasm, fresh ideas of how to improve the work system, and insight about his own management skills were all outcomes of these conversations (Weisbord, 2004). Based on these outcomes, one can view this as an OD coaching conversation between a consultant and client, full of questions, self-evaluation, and suggestions for new concepts and models.

Two important aspects of Weisbord's experience deserve to be mentioned. First, the OD consultant can find value in the coaching intervention. Second, coaching as an individual intervention in turn can help with a larger group intervention.

Warner Burke describes an example of a historical instance of coaching (Burke, 2008). In this scenario, coaching is exemplified as an alternative label for counseling. The example he introduces shows an introductory use of counseling in an organization as part of the research follow-up conducted in the Hawthorne studies (King, 1999). The study was in the Bank wiring observation room. In this study the researchers shifted, intentionally, their role and behavior from researcher to counselor, which was their educational background. Burke (2008) correctly notes that the behaviors that the researchers intentionally used in their conversations with the employees were coaching behaviors. Behaviors such as listening both to what is stated and what is not stated, not giving advice, and paying attention to the emotions around topics discussed by the employees are all coaching behaviors. However, Burke's conclusion that coaches and counselors are the same is questionable. Schein (1988) proposes, in the theory of process consultation that a consultant follows the client's agenda (Burke, 2008). Furthermore, the researchers in the cited study were not coaches because they were not carrying out the client's agenda but rather their own agenda (International Coach Federation, 2017).

Burke and Nourmair (2015) further describe coaching as part of the domain of OD. Coaching can be viewed as a role with its own professional identity as well as one of the most important roles of the OD consultant when working within an organization (Burke & Noumair, 2015). One can identify a direct alignment between the OD values and the ICF coaching competencies. The five OD values are respect and inclusion, collaboration, authenticity, self-awareness, and empowerment. Respect and inclusion stand for equitable values, perspective, and opinions of everyone. Collaboration is what builds collaborative relationships between the practitioner and the client while encouraging collaboration throughout the client system. Authenticity strives for authenticity and congruence and encourages these qualities in their clients. Self-awareness commits to developing self-awareness and interpersonal skills. OD practitioners engage in personal and professional development through lifelong learning. Empowerment focuses efforts on helping all those in the client organization or community to increase their autonomy to levels that make the workplace or community satisfying and productive.

As discussed in Chapter 1, the four ICF competency categories are setting the foundation, co-creating the relationship, communicating effectively, and learning and results. Setting the foundation includes meeting ethical guidelines and professional standards and establishing the coaching agreement. Co-creating the relationship includes establishing trust and intimacy with the client and coaching presence. Communicating effectively includes active listening, powerful questioning, and direct communication. Learning and results include creating awareness, designing actions, planning and goal setting, and managing progress and accountability (International Coach Federation, 2017).

As depicted in Table 2.2, respect and inclusion align with setting the foundation in the sense that rapport is the foundation for a relationship and that understanding the values, perspectives, and opinions of the client helps to establish a partnership. Collaboration and authenticity align with

TABLE 2.2 Coaching and OD Values

OD Values	Alignment	ICF: Coaching Competencies
Respect and inclusion—equitably values the perspective and opinions of everyone.	Rapport is the foundation for a relationship and understanding the values, perspectives, and opinions of your client helps to establish a partnership.	Setting the foundation 1.Meeting ethical guidelines and professional standards 2.Establishing the coaching agreement
Collaboration—builds collaborative relationships between the practitioner and the client while encouraging collaboration throughout the client system.	OD consulting and coaching promotes collaboration and discovery. The client and the practitioner are a team. "Presence" or "being" is the way we are with the client; it is our stated and unstated intention. How we enter a conversation with a client will be mirrored back to us by the client thus affecting the outcome.	1. Establishing trust and intimacy with the client 2.Coaching presence
Authenticity—strives for authenticity and congruence and encourages these qualities in their clients	The OD values highlight the responsibility of the practitioner to be a life-long learner committing to the development of self-awareness and interpersonal skills. The coaching competencies have a similar mantra, but it is directed toward the development of self-awareness and interpersonal skills in the client as a side order to the desired outcome.	Communicating effectively 1.Active listening 2.Powerful questioning 3.Direct communication
Self-awareness—commits to developing self-awareness and interpersonal skills. OD practitioners engage in personal and professional development through lifelong learning.	The assumption of the coach and the OD practitioner is that the clients are the experts on themselves and capable of coming to their own solutions and actions. Both roles respectfully challenge and request action of the client based on the goal stated at the onset of the intervention.	Facilitating learning and results 1.Creating awareness 2.Designing actions 3.Planning and goal setting 4.Managing progress and accountability

cocreating the relationship in the sense that OD consulting and coaching promote interaction and discovery; the client and the practitioner are a team. Presence or being is the way we are with the client; it is our stated and unstated intention. How a conversation is entered with a client will be mirrored back to us by the client, thus affecting the outcome. Self-awareness aligns with communicating effectively in the sense that the OD values highlight the responsibility of the practitioner to be a lifelong learner committing to the development of self-awareness and interpersonal skills. The coaching competencies have a similar mantra but are directed toward the development of self-awareness and interpersonal skills in the client as a side order to the desired outcome. Empowerment aligns with facilitating learning and development in the sense that the assumption of the coach and the OD practitioner is that the clients are the experts on themselves and capable of coming to their own solutions and actions. Both roles respectfully challenge and request action of the client based on the goal stated at the onset of the intervention (International Coach Federation, 2017).

Coaching Specialties

Coaching is an overarching profession that has a number of specialties. The subcategories or specialties of coaching can best be defined by the types of events or issues that are focused on in the coaching engagement. It can be helpful to elucidate the reasons that people might choose to engage with a coach within those different contexts. For example:

Life Coaching

Life coaching is one of the broadest coaching contexts, as it could focus on presenting topics anywhere within the realm of a client's life. Life coaching aids individuals in finding direction, balance, and fulfillment in any one of many different areas of their life. Life coaching has acquired an increasing number of subcategories as well as health coaching, relationship coaching, financial coaching, and so on.

Business Coaching

Business coaching is also a bit of a catchall term but it focuses on coaching in the arena of the workplace. It is often centered on the development of the business or the business objectives. Like other types of coaching, business coaching is focused on forward looking results, however, business coaching is specifically focused on the results of a business or workplace.

Career Coaching

Oftentimes, the career coach has some specific expertise or knowledge in pathways and processes for individuals to explore different career choices. A typical career coach will use a number of different questionnaires and assessments to help the client understand their direction and career preferences.

Executive Coaching

Having an eye toward not only personal goals but also the strategic interests of the organization is a common underpinning of executive coaching. Indeed, Williams (2007) argues, "Two factors distinguish executive coaching from other kinds [of coaching]: It always involves a partnership between the executive, the coach, and the organization; and the individual goals must link back and be integrated into strategic organizational objectives" (p. 1). Stern (2004) similarly states that what drives the coaching are "the needs and preferences of the executive and the organization" (p. 155). He points out that executive coaching is "individualized leadership development, behavior modification, business planning, and organizational re-engineering" (Stern, 2004, p. 157). Stern (2004) says that the difference between executive coaching and other types of coaching "is its dual focus on working one-on-one to develop the executive as a leader while also helping that leader to achieve business results" (p. 157).

Executive coaching benefits not only the individual but also the organization. Regardless of the exact wording of the definition, the goal of executive coaching is to "improve an individual's performance in the workplace" (Johnson, 2007, p. 4).

The Use of Professional Coaching

Coaching is on the rise and an important reason for the growth in the popularity of professional coaching is that coaching affords executives an opportunity to work on issues that would normally get lost in the busy, high-pressure environment and hustle of everyday work life. Rotenberg (2000) addresses the complex roles executives are expected to take on in the middle of ever-increasing pressures to enhance their individual as well as overall company performance. Similarly, Lowman (2005) discusses the "high intensity stress faced by executives, including competing demands among work–life balance, workplace dysfunction, and continual organizational changes" (p. 157). Coaching highlights such issues, allowing the executive to be attentive to them throughout the course of daily work. Schlosser, Steinbrenner, Kumata, and Hunt (2006) agree that "executives must be both strategic decision makers as well as experts in employing soft skills as they manage people" (p. 74). Additionally, this is all done in the context of ambiguity, many changes, and unlimited pressures to increase performance as well as success.

Coaching Outcomes

The true evolution of coaching can be seen in the evidence of success from coaching studies that showcase the powerful results that coaching can create. Ultimately, coaching is driven by the business needs and preferences of both the executive and the organization (Stern, 2004). Natale and Diamante (2005) identify numerous positive benefits of coaching: achievement of personal and professional goals, increased sales, enhanced employee satisfaction, better organizational communication, greater self-knowledge, ability to lead change more effectively, and capacity to make quicker and better decisions. Many companies "lack a disciplined approach to managing the coaching process and measuring outcomes" (McDermott et al., 2007, p. 35).

Another complication is the vast variety of reasons that a person hires a coach, making it difficult to report on the outcomes and success of coaching in general. As Greif (2007) points out: "A fundamental difficulty of coaching outcome research is the extreme heterogeneity of issues, problems and goals, which can be picked out as themes in different coaching interventions. Therefore, it is difficult to identify outcome measures which are applicable to the whole range of coaching interventions" (p. 224). However, some studies do show the results of coaching. Let's look at five examples:

Study 1

Research from the Corporate Leadership Council (2013) indicates that "coaching can provide a high return-on-investment (ROI) and satisfaction rate" (CLC, 2013). For example, the council cites a study conducted by Metrix Global, LLC on a Fortune 500 telecommunications firm that reported an ROI of 529%. Other research conducted by Wasylyshyn (2003) indicates the following outcomes of successful coaching: 63% sustained behavior change, 48% increased self-awareness and understanding, and 45% more effective leadership.

Study 2

A study by McGovern et al. (2001) on the impact of executive coaching shows both the intangible and tangible results of coaching. The researchers studied 100 executives from 56 organizations of various sizes. The results showed that 43% of the companies were able to identify the return on investment of coaching. According to McGovern et al. (2001), "The majority of the 43 participants... reported between $100,000 and $1 million as the return on investment in executive coaching" (p. 7). Additionally, 75% of the sample rated the value of the coaching as "considerably greater" or "far greater" than the money and time spent (McGovern et al., 2001, p. 7). Furthermore, 73% of the study participants indicated they had reached their goals, "very effectively" or "extremely effectively" (McGovern et al., 2001, p. 8). The rate of results was shown to be higher for intangible impacts (i.e., improved relationships with direct reports at 77%, improved teamwork at 67%, improved job satisfaction at 63%) than for tangible ones (i.e., productivity at 53%, quality at 48%, customer service at 39%). As impressive as these numbers may sound, one should keep in mind that this study surveyed the clients of the consulting firm to which the authors belong, and the outcomes are based on estimates by the client (Fillery-Travis & Lane, 2006). On the other hand, certain factors were put into place to enhance reliability; in particular, the data was collected by trained independent contractors, and limits were put on outlier ROI estimates of $1 million (McGovern et al., 2001).

Study 3

In another study aimed at identifying ROI, Phillips (1996) reports that Nations Hotel Corporation (NHC) instituted a formal, structured executive coaching program that NHC then evaluated among 25 randomly selected participants. NHC used Kirkpatrick's (1959) levels of evaluation to assess the program. Based on Level 1 evaluation (reaction), the average rating was 4.1 on a 5-point scale (1 = *unaccep*table, 5 = *exceptional*). Learning (Level 2 evaluation) was assessed by means of a questionnaire given to the coach and client in which enhancement of skills and knowledge was gauged. To assess application of the behavior (Level 3 evaluation), the executive had to create three action plans and then implement them. The action plans contained details on what the executive would do in order to drive a particular item. Among the executive coaches, 83% reported completion of all three action plans, while another 11% completed one or two of them (Phillips, 1996). In addition, the clients and coaches completed a questionnaire about changes in the executive clients' behavior as a result of using these skills. To measure results (Level 4 evaluation), at the beginning of the engagement the clients were required to align their performance goals with at least five measures (productivity-efficiency, sales, direct cost savings, employee retention, and customer satisfaction). The study concluded that the total performance value among the executives was estimated at $1,861,158. The cost of coaching all 25 executives was $579,800.

Study 4

Collecting data beyond dollars and cents is another method of viewing the results of coaching. Starting in December 2004, Cambria Consulting began an ongoing study of the effects of executive coaching in large organizations from the perspective of multiple stakeholders (coach, client, managers as sponsors, and others). They used two methods to assess stakeholders' perceptions. The first was a set of 10 questions regarding the perceived overall benefit of the coaching. The second was that stakeholders were asked to estimate the dollar value using specified ranges for various coaching outcomes. The study assessed these perceptions at the onset and conclusion of the coaching engagement. Of the 132 coaching triads (client, coach, and manager) invited to participate, 95 did. In order to assess the outcomes, respondents selected from a set of results or metrics that were believed to have manifested from the coaching engagement. Across the triads, two items were noted in the top five metric responses from each of the stakeholders (client, coach, and manager): "employee engagement" and "promotion/promotability" (Schlosser et al., 2006, p. 11). In order to assess the perception of value, the three members (coach, client, and manager) responded to a questionnaire with a rating scale from 1 (very little) to 10 (very much). Across the 10 questions, responses from the manager were all lower than those of the coach and client, with the exception of one question: "To what extent (was the manager) personally committed to the coaching process with regard to the client?" (Schlosser et al., 2006, p. 21). Here, the managers rated this an 8.2, clients rated it an 8.3, and coaches a 7.8. In response to the summary question—"At present, how satisfied are you with the value of coaching initiatives across company?"—the average rating for coaches was 8.8 ($SD = 1.1$; $n = 62$) and 7.8 for clients ($SD = 1.7$; $n = 44$) (Schlosser et al., 2006). However, the average rating from managers was 5.3 ([$SD = 2.5$; $n = 12$]; Schlosser et al., 2006). These numbers indicate that coaches and clients perceived the coaching engagement to have higher value estimations than did the managers. In fact, over 85% of the 56 responding coaches and 91% of the 51 responding clients estimated an overall value of $50,000 during the 18-month coaching process. In contrast,

30% of the 12 responding managers did not observe value from the coaching, 42% estimated less than $50,000 in value, and 25% estimated more than $1 million in value.

Study 5

A study on a smaller scale was conducted by Stevens (2005), who interviewed 7 top management executives representing a range of industries (industrial manufacturing, financial services, health care, and academia). The executives also had received coaching. Of the 7 participants, 3 had previously been engaged in a coaching relationship with Stevens. Of those 3 executives, 2 had experiences with other executive coaches, and the remainder of the 7 had had a coach at some time. All the executives had had a coach during their time as a CEO or president of their respective companies. Stevens (2005) found that the executives view coaching as a "helping process wherein something is done with them in a way that also enables them to better meet their role obligations and responsibilities" (p. 283).

Beyond tangible measurements such as cost savings, reduced turnover, and increased productivity, the results of coaching are often based on the intangible. In fact, Fillery-Travis and Lane (2006) pointedly ask, "Is it sufficient that the client perceives coaching to have enabled him/her to achieve an identified goal or does the output have to percolate down to the bottom-line in terms of a quantifiable performance measure for the organization" (p. 29)? As previously discussed, Phillips' (1996) report of NHC's coaching program revealed several intangible benefits that were identified through a questionnaire and action plans. Measures that were identified by at least 4 of the 25 executives as intangible outputs included increased commitment, improved teamwork, increased job satisfaction, improved customer service, and improved communication.

Schlosser et al. (2006) concur that the value generated from coaching is not always a tangible measurement when they say, "Value is in the eyes of the beholder" (p. 3). Schlosser et al. (2006) indicate that the decision makers within an organization look for value creation when determining how to proceed with executive coaching. The authors point out that this value creation is both implicit and explicit, suggesting that costs are not the only factor when evaluating whether executive coaching is the appropriate intervention. Schlosser et al. (2006) also state that ROI is an organization-specific metric, at least in part. Thus, they contend that any metrics should relate to what is important or valued within a given organization: "This perspective … is aligned with the trend toward viewing executive coaching as serving a strategic rather than remedial role" (p. 10). According to

Schlosser et al. (2006), organizations that look beyond the financial impact and returns of coaching into value creation will generally take into account the following company issues and needs: (a) competencies (i.e., behaviors and abilities) necessary of leaders and clients for the execution of business strategy, especially the competencies needed for considerable impact on short and long-term results; (b) individual leaders who largely need these competencies; and (c) ways in which expert coaching can facilitate building these important competencies with these leaders and clients, as they are likely to have noteworthy impact on business results.

Chapter Summary

This chapter has taken a look at the origins of coaching. It has grown from a rogue and unstandardized process to a profession with proven results and a credentialing process. Upon exploring the history of the coaching intervention as it has grown into a profession, it is evident that coaching has a connection to the business world and truly started to define itself in the 1980s. Its roots clearly define its strong ties to the OD field as a very positive-focused development tool. Lastly, there are many examples of coaching success outlined in this chapter.

Chapter Reflection Questions

1. How does the history of coaching play into its perception by the general public?
2. What is the value of the profession of coaching having roots from so many different disciplines and bodies of knowledge?
3. How do you feel organizations that you have been a part of would be able to benefit from coaching?

Activity

How would you explain the benefit of coaching to a current or past organization that you have been a part of? What would be the value proposition? How would you leverage coaching's powerful history and roots to explain and showcase its relevance and value?

References

Axmith, M. (2004). Executive coaching: A catalyst for personal growth and corporate change. *Ivey Business Journal, May/June,* 1–5.

Burke, W. W. (2008). *Organizational change: Theory and practice* (2nd ed.). Thousand Oaks, CA: SAGE.

Burke, W., & Noumair, D. (2015). *Organization development: A process of learning and changing* (3rd ed.). Indianapolis, IN: Pearson FT Press.

Corporate Leadership Council. (2013). [Summary of research: Executive coaching]. Unpublished raw data.

Fillery-Travis, A., & Lane, D. (2006). Does coaching work or are we asking the wrong question? *International Coaching Psychology Review, 1*(1), 23–36.

Greif, S. (2007). Advances in research on coaching outcomes. *International Coaching Psychology Review, 2*(3), 222–242.

Harris, M. (1999). Look, it's an I-O psychologist no, it's a trainer . . . no, it's an executive coach. *TIP, 36*(3), 1–5.

International Coach Federation. (2017). Coaching core competencies. Retrieved from http://www.coachfederation.org/ICF/For+Current+Members/ Credentialing/Why+a+Credential/Competencies/

Johnson, L. K. (2007). Getting more from executive coaching. *Harvard Management Update,* January, 3–6.

Judge, W. Q., & Cowell, J. (1997). The brave new world of executive coaching. *Business Horizons, 40*(4), 71–77.

Kilburg, R. R. (1996). Toward a conceptual understanding and definition of executive coaching. *Consulting Psychology Journal: Practice and Research, 48*(2), 134–144.

King, P., & Eaton, J. (1999). *Coaching for results. Industrial and Commercial Training, 31*(4), 145–148.

Kirkpatrick, D. (1959). Techniques for evaluating training programs. *Journal of the American Society for Training and Development, 13*(11), 3–9.

Lowman, R. (2005). Executive coaching: The road to dodoville needs paving with more than good assumptions. *Consulting Psychology Journal: Practice and Research, 57*(1), 90–96.

McDermott, M., Levenson, A., & Newton, S. (2007). What coaching can and cannot do for your organization. *Human Resource Planning, 30*(2), 30–37.

McGovern, J., Lindemann, M., Vergara, M., Murphy, S., Barker, L., & Warrenfeltz, R. (2001). Maximizing the impact of executive coaching: Behavioral change, organizational outcomes, and return on investment. *The Manchester Review, 6*(1), 1–9.

Natale, S. M., & Diamante, T. (2005). The five stages of executive coaching: Better process makes better practice. *Journal of Business Ethics, 59,* 361–374.

Phillips, J. J. (1996). Measuring the ROI of a coaching intervention, part 2. *Performance Improvement, 46*(10), 10–23.

Rotenberg, C. T. (2000). Psychodynamic psychotherapy and executive coaching: Overlapping paradigms. *Journal of the American Academy of Psychoanalysis, 28*, 653–663.

Schein, E. H. (1988). *Organizational culture and leadership.* San Francisco, CA: Jossey-Bass.

Schlosser, B., Steinbrenner, D., Kumata, E., & Hunt, J. (2006). The coaching impact study: Measuring the value of executive coaching. *International Journal of Coaching in Organizations, 4*(3), 8–26.

Stern, L. R. (2004). Executive coaching: A working definition. *Consulting Psychology Journal: Practice and Research, 56*(3), 154–162.

Stevens, J. H., Jr. (2005). Executive coaching from the executive's perspective. *Consulting Psychology Journal: Practice and Research, 57*(4), 274–285.

Tobias, L. L. (1996). Coaching executives. *Consulting Psychology Journal: Practice and Research, 48*(2), 87–95.

Wasylyshyn, K. M. (2003). Executive coaching: An outcome study. *Consulting Psychology Journal: Practice and Research, 55*(2), 94–106.

Weisbord, M. R. (2004). *Productive workplaces revisited: Dignity, meaning, and community in the 21st century.* San Francisco, CA: Jossey-Bass.

Williams, R. (2007). *The second-fastest growing profession.* Retrieved February 29, 2008 from http://www.coachfederation.org/

3

The Different Models of Coaching

This chapter explores the value of various coaching models. Many coaches learn and practice a number of different models in their coaching. Models can be considered tools in a coach's toolbox that can be drawn upon based on the needs of the individual client. As you discover and learn about the different models, it helps to "try them on" and practice them to see which fits your coaching style and your client's needs the best. As we look at each model, the relationship between each model and the coaching outcomes will be examined. The models presented in this chapter are the most well-known, utilized, and researched models that are used in effective coaching engagements.

Why Models?

To begin to address this question about why we use models, it helps to revisit our definition of coaching from Chapter 1:

An Introduction to Professional and Executive Coaching, pages 37–54
Copyright © 2018 by Information Age Publishing
All rights of reproduction in any form reserved.

> Effective coaching is a transformational process where the coach is the cata-
> lyst and the client gains awareness around solutions, answers, and shifts that
> will help them to achieve goals and reach a state of thriving.

The definition discusses process. The coaching process is the lifeblood of
an effective and productive coaching engagement, in the sense that there is
a framework to draw upon. However, as these models provide a framework
for effective coaching, it is important to remember that they are just that, a
framework. They are not a rigid structure that does not allow for flexibility.
They allow for the client to be met where they are. An additional benefit of
models is that they create an evidence-based process that can be described
and explained, and can contribute to the measurement of outcomes of
coaching.

The Different Models of Coaching

The art of coaching comes in many forms and specialties. Specifically, this
section reviews solutions-focused coaching, appreciative inquiry coaching
(AIC), alignment coaching, co-active coaching, the GROW model, CLEAR
model, and neuro-linguistic programming.

Solutions-Focused Coaching

The solutions-focus process is a powerful, practical, and proven approach to positive change with people, teams, and organizations. With this
approach, the search for the causes of problems is sidestepped. The focus is
on solutions and strengths and on what is going well. This process leads to a
positive and pragmatic way of making progress (Axmith, 2004).

Solution-focused coaching comes from brief therapy, which was developed in the early 1980s by a research group in Milwaukee including Insoo
Kim Berg and Steve de Shazer. The group wanted to find something effective and efficient to help clients start successfully doing whatever it was that
they were striving for in their lives. They began to experiment with a "what
might work" perspective and framework instead of using a "what caused
the problem" perspective or framework. By focusing on and building upon
solutions, they were able to reduce their average consultation time by over
70% while still retaining the same success rate as the other forms of therapy.
In 1997, Peter Szabó started to transfer these findings to the world of coaching. The result is what we know today as solution-focused coaching.

Perhaps, the key contribution of brief therapy to solution-focused coaching has been the miracle question (see Figure 3.1). The miracle question is

> Suppose tonight, when you are fast asleep, a miracle happens
> and all the problems that brought you here today are solved just like that.
> But since the miracle happened overnight, nobody is telling you
> that the miracle is happened. When you wake up the next morning,
> how are you going to start discovering that the miracle happened?
> ...What else are you going to notice? What else?

Figure 3.1   The miracle question. *Source:* de Shazer & Berg, 1995.

a great example of the principles of solutions-focused coaching in that the focus is on the future and the solution. According to Jackson and McKergow (2008), the solutions-focused model is based on the 6 SIMPLE principles:

1. *Solutions, not problems.* The coach keeps the conversation on the solutions and not on the problems. This does not mean ignoring problems, but rather looking at them in the context of what the client would like instead.
2. *Not the individual—the action is in the interaction.* Each coaching conversation is creating a new and joint interaction between the coach and client. As a coach, you are looking for new ways to move forward in each conversation.
3. *Make use of what's there, not what isn't.* Observe and illuminate what the client already possesses in their own ideas, strengths, and abilities.
4. *Possibilities—past, present, and future.* As a coach, one of your most important objectives is to inspire a sense of possibility.
5. *Language—clear, not complicated.* The coach accepts, restates, and reflects the client's language back to them in the coaching conversation.
6. *Every case is different.* Beware of an ill-fitting theory. Not only is each client different but each coaching conversation with each client is different. It is important for the coach to come to each conversation with new curiosity.

At the most basic level, the solution-focused coaching model focuses on:

- ▪ *Don't fix what isn't broken.* Focus on what the client wants to be different instead.
- ▪ *Find what works, and do more of it.* Find the exceptions to the problem, when things are working well, while noting that when the solution is happening already, whether spontaneously, by accident, or even only in part, these exceptions can be replicated.

- *Stop doing what doesn't work, and do something else.* Sometimes the solution to the problem can become a problem itself—a kind of vicious circle that we need to break out of. When something isn't working, try something else.
- *Exploring Solutions.* Use available energy and time solely for exploring solutions that move toward the future rather than exploring the past. To fully operate within the solutions-focused model, the goal is to find out what is working and to do more of that while stopping what isn't working or doing less or none of that.
- *Illuminating Resources. Ask about and uncover competences and skills.* We assume that all skills necessary to master a situation or work through a problem are already present within the client. It is not about hiding deficits but instead it is about illuminating existing strengths, behaviors, and skills and using them to work towards a solution.
- *Find new perspectives.* Change the focus of your awareness. Change the focus of your awareness to something new.

OSKAR Model

The OSKAR framework is extensively borrowed from solution-focused methodology (see Figure 3.2). It was developed in the 1970s by Steve de Shazer and Kim Berg and their team (de Shazer & Berg, 1995). This work developed the idea of scaling questions to ask clients where they rate themselves on a scale of 1 to 10 based on their skill, thought, emotion, progress, and so on.

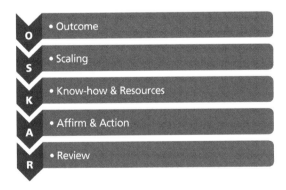

Figure 3.2 OSKAR model. *Source:* de Shazer & Berg, 1995.

Examples of coaching questions for each stage of the OSKAR model:

Outcome

- What is the objective of this coaching?
- What do you want to achieve today?
- What do you want to achieve in the long term?
- How will you know this coaching has been of use to you?
- What is the perfect version of the future?

Scaling

- On a scale of 0 to 10, with 10 representing the future perfect and 0 the worst it has ever been, where are you on that scale today?
- You are at (stated number) now: What did you do to get this far?
- How would you know that you have gotten to an (stated number) +1?

Know-How and Resources

- What helps you perform at a/an (stated number) on the scale, rather than 0?
- When does the outcome already happen for you, even a little bit?
- What did you do to make it happen? How did you do that?
- What did you do differently?
- What would other people say you are doing well?

Affirm and Action

- What's already going well?
- What is the next small step? What would you like to do personally, straight away?
- You are at a/an (stated number) now, what would it take to get you to a/an (stated number) +1?

Review

- What's better?
- What did you do that made the change happen?
- What effects have the changes had?
- What do you think will change next?

Appreciative Inquiry (AI) Coaching

According to Gordon (2008), "Appreciative Inquiry came to life in the 1980s, and has been evolving ever since as a positive philosophical and practical approach to organizational change" (p. 212). AI is based on five principles: constructionist, poetic, simultaneity, anticipatory, and positive. There are also emerging principles: wholeness, enactment, free choice, awareness, and narrative. Gordon states that the aim is to focus on the strengths and the positive core of an organization.

Cooperrider and Whitney (2005) define AI in these terms:

> Appreciative Inquiry is about the coevolutionary search for the best in people, their organizations, and the relevant world around them. In its broadest focus, it involves systematic discovery of what gives "life" to a living system when it is most alive, most effective, and most constructively capable in economic, ecological, and human terms. AI involves, in a central way, the art and practice of asking questions that strengthen a system's capacity to apprehend, anticipate and heighten positive potential. (p. 17)

Likewise, coaching using AI focuses clients on the positive present and the possibilities of the future, rather than the problems of the present and past. In short, Sloan and Canine (2007) say that, AI coaching means simply applying the core AI principles with a client in a practical manner. At the heart of AI is that "human systems are heliotropic in that they gravitate to what resides in their inner most being, which are their values, vision, accomplishments, and best self" (p. 27).

Orem, Binkert, and Clancy (2007) developed an AIC model that includes the following elements: (a) something works in every society, organization, group, or person; (b) reality is determined by what one focuses upon; (c) there are multiple realities and they are created in the moment; (d) asking a question of another (an organization, team, or individual) influences the other in some manner; (e) if individuals bring portions of their past to the present, these should be the best from the past; and (f) reality is created by the language one uses.

The foundation of AIC is "built upon the assumption that within every person something works and what a person focuses upon becomes their reality. To facilitate this foundational concept, appreciative rather than problem-solving questions are asked in AIC" (Gordon, 2008, p. 73). Examples of these differences, according to Gordon (2008), include the following questions: "Tell me what the problem is?"; "What gives you energy?"; "What worries you?"; "What do you want more of?"; "What's bothering you?"; "What's working well now?"; "What do you think is the cause?"; and "How do you wish to continue moving forward?" (p. 25).

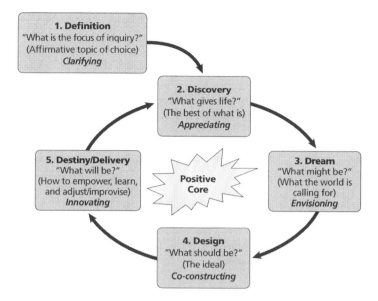

Figure 3.3 5D model of AIC. *Source:* Orem et al., 2007.

The 5-D Model of AIC (Figure 3.3) consists of:

- *Definition.* Define the focus of the coaching.
- *Discovery.* Appreciate "what is."
- *Dream.* Imagine "what might be."
- *Design.* Determine "what should be."
- *Destiny.* Create what "will be."

Examples of questions for each stage of the AIC model:

Definition—Define the Focus of the Coaching

- What gives you life now?
- Describe a high point of peak experiences.
- What do you most value about . . . ?
- What do you want more of in your life?

Discovery

- Coach asks client to describe a positive experience.
- The client reflects the positive elements of that experience.
- The coach and the client identify similarities across multiple positive experiences.
- The client applies learnings to the coaching topic.

Dream

- If you could have three wishes, what would they be?
- Think about the times you were most happy. What about these times would you want to carry into the future?
- What do you notice about yourself when you dream of your future?

Design

- Think about your dream. What will make it come alive for you?
- What in your dream really calls to you and makes you yearn for its fulfillment?
- What have you done before that you could do again to move forward in the future?

Destiny—Create What "Will Be"

- What commitments do you want to make to yourself?
- How will you continue to foster growth, progress, and development?
- What do you want to do more of to get closer to your dream?

Alignment Coaching

Alignment coaching is intended to help clients understand their values, beliefs, and expectations (Lazar & Bergquist, 2004). This coaching type focuses on helping the client think about how his or her values affect or contribute to their perspective on the world, in order to understand what is important. Alignment coaching helps clients become clear about the match or mismatch between a client's values and the organization. According to Lazar and Bergquist (2004), alignment coaching consists of four coaching subcategories: spiritual, philosophical, ethics, and life and career. Spiritual coaching focuses on reflection, appreciation, and contemplation of transcendent forces. It also has a focus on the meaning of people's lives.

Although philosophical coaching is similar, the goal is to shed light on a client's beliefs and assumptions and how they can impact perception. Ethics coaching works with the clients to clarify their ethical viewpoints and stances. It gives clients the opportunity to explore whether these betray or align with their personal ethics and values. The ethics coach also supports the client as they seek alignment among his or her personal and professional life, family and community, personal interests, and collective societal responsibilities. In life and career coaching, the coaching looks at the entire life experience of the client. Many issues can be covered such as financial, friendship, time for leisure, and career goals. Oftentimes, assessments, powerful questions, and planning exercises are used in life and career coaching.

The areas of coaching that benefit the most from alignment coaching are

- spiritual coaching,
- philosophical coaching,
- ethics coaching, and
- life and career coaching.

Co-Active Coaching

Whitworth, Kimsey-House & Sandahl (2010) describe the co-active coaching model as a proven approach based on many years of experience in working with clients (see Figure 3.4). The four cornerstones of co-active coaching are as follows: The client is naturally creative, resourceful, and whole; the agenda comes from the client; the coach dances in the moment; and co-active coaching addresses the client's whole life. It is a collaborative and dynamic partnership between coach and client that involves full participation from both parties.

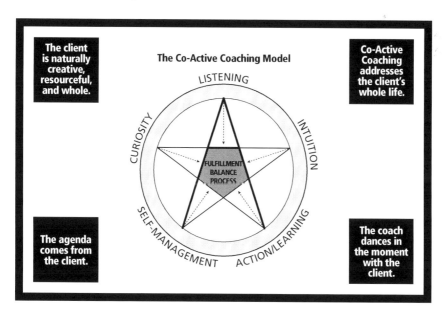

Figure 3.4 The co-active coaching model. *Source:* Whitworth et al., 2010.

The first cornerstone means that the client has the answer and the ability to find it. In this sense, the coach does not have the answer; rather it is the client who does. The coach simply asks the questions to help spark the answer. From this viewpoint, the coach is not there to fix the client because the client is not broken. Rather, it is a matter of helping the client uncover the answers he or she is seeking.

The second cornerstone means that the relationship is focused on the results the client wishes to experience. Additionally, during the coach–client relationship, the client makes changes in his or her life, and the coach continues to maintain focus on the client's overall agenda so that it does not get lost or overlooked. Thus, the coach ensures that the client continues to navigate toward fulfillment and shifting perspectives. The third cornerstone means that the coach is always open to the client's agenda and where he or she needs to be at that time. The last cornerstone (the client's whole life is addressed) stems from the belief that all of the client's choices and behaviors contribute to a life that is more fulfilling (Whitworth et al., 2010).

The co-active coaching model is depicted as a star with each of the five points representing one of the five contexts of listening, intuition, curiosity, action/learning, and self-management. In this model, these five contexts represent what the coach brings to the coaching relationship as a point of contact with the client. The coach consistently draws upon each of these contexts during coaching. None of these contexts are in a specific order or more important than another and each serves the process to support the client in achieving balance and fulfillment.

GROW Model of Coaching

Perhaps one of the most well recognized coaching models that evolved in the 1990s is the GROW model. The GROW model is appreciated for its simplicity and straightforwardness. This model is a framework that was commercialized by Sir John Whitmore. He is known for his ability to align the coaching process to ethical practice to better develop people as opposed to solely impact a business's bottom line. The GROW model consists of four stages (Whitmore, 2009).

- *Goals.* Goal setting for the session.
- *Reality.* Checking to explore the current situation.
- *Options.* Options and alternative strategies or course of action.
- *Will/Wrap-Up.* What is to be done, when, and by whom?

The sequence of the model assumes that it is important to spend time in all four stages. The GROW model is effective because of its simplicity as well as its focus on helping clients to uncover unconscious motivations which might prevent them from reaching their goals.

Goal

- What do you want to achieve from this coaching session?
- What goal do you want to achieve?
- What would you like to happen with _____?
- What do you really want?

Reality

- What is happening now (what, who, when, and how often)? What is the effect or result of this?
- How would you describe what you did?
- Where are you now in relation to your goal?
- On a scale of one to ten, where are you?

Options

- What are your options?
- What do you think you need to do next?
- What could be your first step?
- What do you think you need to do to get a better result (or closer to your goal)?

Will/Wrap-Up

- How are going to go about it?
- What do you think you need to do right now?
- How will you know when you have done it?
- Is there anything else you can do?

CLEAR Model

This model was designed by Peter Hawkins (Hawkins & Smith, 2006) and came from his background in therapy, supervision and organizational management (see Figure 3.5).

Contracting

It is a unique aspect of this model to begin with this important stage. Contracting, in essence, is about questions: "What is our goal?"; "Why are

Figure 3.5 CLEAR model. *Source:* Hawkins & Smith, 2006.

we here?"; "What will we do?"; "Who will do it?"; "How will we do it?"; and "How often?"

Listening

Along with using the appropriate interventions, listening helps the coach to assist the client in putting together a clear and accurate representation of their world, their goals, and their insights.

Exploring

Hawkins (Hawkins & Smith, 2006) uses exploring to represent two things: (a) Looking at the impact of the current situation on the client and (b) exploring possibilities to move forward and generate action.

Action

This involves working with the client to take forward-moving action toward achieving his or her desired outcomes and goals.

Review

In this stage of the model, the client reviews what has changed for them, what shifts or insights they have made, and what they will do or do differently going forward.

Neuro Linguistic Programming in Coaching

Neuro linguistic programming (NLP) is more of a process than a model, however, the understanding and practice of NLP can transform the coaching process. NLP is a relationship between mental processes, language, and conditioning. It can be used to better understand how we create our own programs, which impact our behavior. In the context of coaching, NLP is being introduced in this book to showcase the value of its specific tools and techniques to contribute to the coaching client's success and progress.

NLP is having a profound impact on the development of the practice of coaching. Today, NLP techniques are starting to be taught within many coaching courses and curriculums without necessarily being labeled as such. This can make it difficult to measure exactly how many coaches are practicing NLP techniques, but it can be estimated that it is a common practice for many coaches. According to the Association for NLP, NLP is underpinned by a set of operating assumptions or principles called "presuppositions" in NLP circles. There is a fascinating degree of overlap and compatibility between the presuppositions used by NLP practitioners and the principles we use in coaching.

The Presuppositions are:

- *Have respect for the other person's model of the world.* We are all unique and experience the world in different ways. Everyone is individual and has his or her own special way of being.
- *The map is not the territory.* People respond to their "map" of reality, not to reality itself. How people make sense of the world around them is through their senses and from their own personal experience; this means that each individual's perception of an event is different.
- *Mind and body form a linked system.* Your mental attitude affects your body and your health and, in turn, how you behave. If what you are doing isn't working, do something else.
- *Flexibility is the key to success.* Choice is better than no choice. Having options can provide more opportunities for achieving results.
- *We are always communicating.* Even when we remain silent, we are communicating. Nonverbal communication can account for a large proportion of a message.
- *The meaning of your communication is the response you get.* While your intention may be clear to you, it is the other person's interpretation and response that reflects your effectiveness. NLP teaches you the skills and flexibility to ensure that the message you send equals the message they receive.
- *There is no failure, only feedback.* What seemed like failure can be thought of as success that just stopped too soon. With this understanding, we can stop blaming ourselves and others, find solutions and improve the quality of what we do.
- *Behind every behavior there is a positive intention.* When we understand that other people have some positive intention in what they say and do (however annoying and negative it may seem to us), it can be easier to stop getting angry and start to move forward.
- *Anything can be accomplished if the task is broken down into small enough steps.* Achievement becomes easier if activities are manage-

able; NLP can help you learn how to analyze what needs to be done and find ways to be both efficient and effective.

The presuppositions are the foundation of NLP that give it its powerful structure. NLP and coaching are a powerful combination that can bring about a greater level of awareness and robust results for the client.

Reasons for Coaching

Just as there are many definitions of coaching, there are many reasons that coaching is used. One reason is the ever-increasing demands being placed on professionals. This is a major factor that has influenced the growth of executive coaching. The myriad of diverse pressures and challenges that professionals face may include increased competition and change. An additional reason for coaching is the relative isolation and loneliness that many executives experience. These circumstances can cause an executive to look for someone whom he or she can trust to provide objectivity, support, and counsel (Sperry, 1993).

Consulting firms started using coaching around 1990 (Judge & Cowell, 1997). Since then, coaching has started to be used more universally. In fact, annual spending in the United States on coaching is thought to be approximately $1 billion (Sherman & Freas, 2004). Additionally, research conducted by the International Coach Federation, indicates that "senior executives highly value professional coaching, ranking it among the top five leadership development interventions" (International Coach Federation, 2017, para. 3). From another perspective, the growth of coaching is exemplified by the number of ICF members, which has risen from 6,791 in 2003 to more than 17,000 in 2017.

As McDermott, Levenson, and Newton (2007) declares, coaching is the second-fastest growing profession in the world, rivaled only by information technology. As a supporting example, they surveyed 55 companies of which 80% were multinational with mean annual sales in 2007 of $18.5 billion and 34,000 employees. Of these companies, 57% indicated they have plans to increase coaching "moderately" or "a lot," and 41% planned to maintain the amount of coaching, while 2% planned to decrease it (McDermott et al., 2007, p. 32). Many companies have integrated coaching into their leadership development programs (McDermott et al., 2007; Reeves, 2006). In fact, research on the development of effective leaders points toward individuals such as coaches who have helped the leader along the way (Boyatzis, Smith, & Blaize, 2006). In an additional study of 55 companies, 24% identified that they provide coaching to their top management team, and

16% identified that coaching is provided to their middle level management team (McDermott et al., 2007). More specifically, coaching is used to bring about team and organizational change through individual intervention (Morgan, Harkins, & Goldsmith, 2005). Unlike other forms of leadership development such as group workshops, it offers a tailored approach that acknowledges and honors the individuality of the client (Stratford & Freas, 2004; Tobias, 1996). Natale and Diamante (2005) state that "executive coaching can be thought of as a collaborative alliance between coach and client aimed at change and transformation" (p. 24). Within the coaching relationship the coach helps the client reach goals and new levels of productivity and success that the client would not be able to reach as quickly alone (Morgan et al., 2005).

The services of a coach are diverse and may include helping to manage stress, meet job requirements, improve interpersonal relations, increase organizational effectiveness, avoid career derailment, manage change more effectively, set priorities, and make difficult decisions (Diedrich, 1996; Hall, Otazo, & Hollenbeck, 1999; Natale & Diamante, 2005). The ultimate goal of coaching is often to benefit the organization as well as the individual. According to Kilburg (2004), "The focus nearly always remains on how to help people [executives] who have already demonstrated a great deal of competence and success get even better at what they do" (p. 204). In simple terms, the reason for coaching is to "allow for ongoing, continuous learning, while offering support, encouragement, and feedback as new approaches are tried and new behaviors practiced" (Tobias, 1996, p. 87). In this manner, the coaches help executives by challenging them toward their potential while addressing resistance. In the end, this process sets the stage for continuous learning and ultimately for change.

Professional coaching may also be used to assist a newly appointed leader to make the transition into a new role or to help prepare a new leader as part of the succession planning process (Axmith, 2004). Coaching can help an individual both professionally and personally. Lukaszewski (1988) and Sperry (1993) agree that executives in their day-to-day role often do not have colleagues they may turn to in order to ask questions, gain advice, or receive counsel on a difficult situation. Sperry (1993) states, "Many senior executives, particularly CEO's, find it necessary to bounce their ideas and concerns off someone in order to clarify their impressions and validate the reasonableness of their conclusion" (p. 262). Thus, coaching is a useful business and personal tool for professionals.

Other reasons executives may engage the services of a coach include to improve their communication style, enhance their interpersonal skills, become more sensitive to and aware of others' feelings, increase confidence, manage work–life balance, and enhance emotional intelligence (Reeves, 2006). Sometimes, there is no specific problem to be addressed, but instead the executive wishes to "enhance his or her style, future options, and organizational impact" (Tobias, 1996, p. 88). On a more individual and personal results level, executive coaching is a window into enhanced self-awareness for the executive that in turn creates the context for him or her to live more consciously and contribute more richly (Sherman & Freas, 2004). The outcomes of executive coaching are supported by a unique aspect of the relationship in that it provides the executive with a safe haven nestled in confidentiality where he or she can delve into self-exploration, self-awareness, and self-improvement with the coach (Reeves, 2006). This can be extremely powerful since, according to Saporito (1996), the higher one moves up in an organization the less feedback one generally receives. Thus, the coach fills a valuable and indispensable void by acting as a confidante and sounding board.

Despite all the reasons for engaging a coach, coaching cannot transform an executive entirely. Saporito (1996) cautions that rarely do executives change their behavior completely, and doing so would be an unfair expected outcome of the coaching engagement. What is hoped for, however, is "getting the individual to modify enough of his or her behavior to fit the specific behavioral requirements and success factors to a great enough degree that he or she can help the company achieve its organizational imperatives" (Saporito, 1996, p. 103).

Chapter Summary

There are many reasons for a client to engage with a coach. It is important for coaches to study and learn as many different models of coaching as possible and then implement the methodologies and models that resonate the most with them and their clients.

Chapter Reflection Questions

1. What models of coaching resonate with you the most and why?
2. How can a coach integrate multiple models into their own coaching process?
3. What are some of the most common reasons for coaching?

Activity

Pick one of the coaching models described in this chapter and design what a coaching conversation might look like. What are some of the questions that would be important to consider for each stage or step of the model? What situations, examples or types of coaching would best fit this chosen model? Are there any situations where the chosen model would not be a good fit?

References

Axmith, M. (2004, May/June). Executive coaching: A catalyst for personal growth and corporate change. *Ivey Business Journal*, 1–5.

Boyatzis, R. E., Smith, M. L., & Blaize, N. (2006). Developing sustainable leaders through coaching and compassion. *Academy of Management Learning and Education*, 5(1), 8–24.

Cooperider, D., & Whitney, D. (2005) *Appreciative Inquiry*. Oakland, CA. Berrett-Koehler Communications.

de Shazer, S., & Berg, K. (1995). The brief therapy tradition. In J. H. Weakland, & A. E. Wendel (Eds.), *Propagations: Thirty years of influence from the Mental Research Institute* (pp. 249–252). Binghamton, NY: The Haworth Press.

Diedrich, R. C. (1996). An iterative approach to executive coaching. *Consulting Psychology Journal: Practice and Research*, 48(2), 61–66.

Gordon, S. (2008). Appreciative inquiry coaching. *International Coaching Psychology Review*, 3(1), 19–31.

Hall, D. T., Otazo, K. L., & Hollenbeck, G. P. (1999). Behind closed doors: What really happens in executive coaching. *Organizational Dynamics*, 27(3), 39–54.

Hawkins, P., & Smith N. (2006). *Coaching, mentoring and organizational consultancy: Supervision and development*. Maidenhead, England: Open University Press.

International Coach Federation. (2017). *How is coaching distinct from other service professions?* Retrieved June 25, 2017 from https://coachfederation.org/faqs

Jackson, P., & McKergow, M. (2008). *The solutions focus*. Boston, MA. Nicholas Brealey International.

Judge, W. Q., & Cowell, J. (1997, July/August). The brave new world of executive coaching. *Business Horizons*, 40, 71–77.

Kilburg, R. (2004). Trudging toward dodoville: Conceptual approaches and case studies in executive coaching. *Consulting Psychology Journal: Practice and Research*, 56(3), 203–213.

Lazar, J., & Bergquist, W. (2004). Alignment coaching: A broader perspective on business coaching. *Performance Improvement*, 43(10), 16–22.

Lukaszewski, J. E. (1988). Behind the throne: How to coach and counsel executives. *Training*, 42(10), 33–35.

McDermott, M., Levenson, A., & Newton, S. (2007). What coaching can and cannot do for your organization. *Human Resource Planning, 30*(2), 30–37.

Morgan, H., Harkins, P., & Goldsmith, M. (Eds.). (2005). *The art and practice of leadership coaching: 50 top executive coaches reveal their secrets.* Hoboken, NJ: Wiley and Sons.

Natale, S. M., & Diamante, T. (2005). The five stages of executive coaching: Better process makes better practice. *Journal of Business Ethics, 59,* 361–374.

Orem, S. L., Binkert, J., & Clancy, A. L. (2007). *Appreciative coaching: A positive process for change.* San Francisco, CA: Jossey-Bass.

Reeves, W. B. (2006). The value proposition for executive coaching. *Financial Executive, 22*(10), 48–49.

Saporito, T. J. (1996). Business-linked executive development: Coaching senior executives. *Consulting Psychology Journal: Practice and Research, 48*(2), 96– 103.

Sherman, S., & Freas, A. (2004). The wild west of executive coaching. *Harvard Business Review, 82*(11), 82–90.

Sloan, B., & Canine, T. (2007, May). Appreciative inquiry coaching: Exploration and learnings. *AI Practitioner: The International Journal of AI Best Practices,* 1–5.

Sperry, L. (1993). Working with executives: Consulting, counseling, and coaching. *Individual Psychology, 49*(2), 257–267.

Stratford, S., & Freas, A. (2004). The wild west of executive coaching. *Harvard Business Review, 82*(11), 82–90.

Tobias, L. L. (1996). Coaching executives. *Consulting Psychology Journal: Practice and Research, 48*(2), 87–95.

Whitmore, J. (2009) *Coaching for performance: Growing human potential and purpose—The principles and practice of coaching and leadership* (4th ed.), London, England: Nicholas Brealey.

Whitworth, L., Kimsey-House, H., & Sandahl, P. (2010). *Co-active coaching: New skills for coaching people toward success in work and life.* Palo Alto, CA: Davies-Black.

4

The Process of Coaching

This chapter will examine the research on the components of a strong coaching process to summarize the important components of the coaching conversation. Coaching is meant to be fluid, however, having a structure in place that can be altered as needed but used as a framework to support the coaching creates an environment of what can be expected and contributes to how the coaching can be assessed and measured. We will also look at the various ways that coaching success can be assessed. Many organizations default to looking at quantitative bottom-line metrics, however, research is mounting to support alternative measures of the value of coaching.

The Process of Coaching

Just as there are multiple iterations of coaching definitions and outcomes, there is also no single and absolute coaching process. However, a general process can be identified in the literature. Perhaps at the heart of this process is the willingness and readiness of the coachee. Johnson (2007) makes

An Introduction to Professional and Executive Coaching, pages 55–66

the point that effective coaching is contingent upon: the coachees identifying their goals, following a meticulous coach selection process, and having a mindset that is willing and ready to learn and change. Coachee motivation is a related facet to this mindset. Peterson (1996) states, "People are motivated to work on their development when they perceive discrepancies between where they are and where they wish to go" (p. 79). Thus, as a condition that supports successful coaching, Axmith (2004) says that the executive must be receptive to new ways of looking at problems and solutions.

Kilburg (1996) adopted principles from Weinberger (1995) that focus on specific outcomes of the coaching process: (a) establishing an intervention agreement, (b) building a coaching relationship, (c) creating and maintaining expectations of success, (d) providing experiences of mastery and cognitive control, and (e) evaluating and attributing coaching successes and failures.

To flesh out these components further, Kilburg (1996) discusses the first element of establishing end goals for the coaching partnership, securing confidentiality, estimating a time commitment, and establishing fees. In the second element, Kilburg (1996) states the need for building an alliance and gaining commitment. He does not specifically expand on the third component, however, this may be considered to be straightforward. The fourth component of the executive coaching process, according to Kilburg (1996), is mastery and cognitive control. This can be exemplified through using coaching techniques and methods with flexibility, problem solving, identifying and understanding emotions, employing feedback and disclosure with maximum effort, and being prepared to confront acting out and moral concerns of ethical misjudgments in a diplomatic manner. The fifth component, according to Kilberg (1996), is to check in on the coaching and to assess the relationship to make sure that it is working well.

Natale and Diamante (2005) present the following stages of coaching: (a) alliance check, (b) credibility assessment, (c) likeability link, (d) dialogue and skill acquisition, and (e) cue-based action plans. For the first step the authors state, "The alliance activates the conversations that will lead to the writing of a roadmap and removal of resistance" (Natale & Diamante, 2005, p. 363). Natale and Diamante (2005) explain that the second stage is "centered on the executive's desire to gain control and determine whether the coach has anything to offer" (p. 36). The third stage occurs as the executive compares his or her style and preferences with that of the coach. The fourth stage, dialogue and skill acquisition, helps prepare the executive for change. The final stage, cue-based action plans, delineates what the executive is to do. This model is based on the premise that the executive is personally accountable for change in that "through self-control (physically, intellectually, emotionally, and behaviorally) the executive contributes to the nature, meaning, importance, and consequences of the event to which he is 'responding'" (Natale & Diamante, 2005, p. 368).

Ting and Scisco (2015) summarize the coaching relationship process in three steps: assessment, feedback on the assessment, and performance monitoring and follow-up sessions. The assessment phase includes administering a variety of tools, followed by a feedback session to agree upon goals and action plans. This is followed by regular follow-ups on a weekly, biweekly, or monthly basis, which may happen in person or over the telephone.

Beginning a coaching engagement with a contract is cited as an important first step in the coaching process. Natale and Diamante (2005) contend that a contract among the coachee, coach, and organization is essential for laying the proper groundwork. According to Natale and Diamante (2005), the contract should include a confidentiality provision, length of service, minimum amount of coaching, means of communication between the coach and coachee, fees, expenses, and method of billing.

Diedrich (1996) states that a contract should be for an extended time frame; specifying that 12 months should be the minimum. He adds that the process and system of coaching used may continuously change throughout the engagement. In terms of confidentiality, Diedrich (1996) recommends discussing what is confidential. He further advocates for occasional review sessions with the coachee, sponsor organization, and coach to assess how the engagement is progressing when the coaching is an engagement inside an organization. Furthermore, he recommends that the contract outlines that the coach should have the opportunity to see the coachee in his work environment, specifically when working with subordinates.

Two aspects of the coaching engagement that require additional attention are confidentiality and trust. Natale and Diamante (2005) identify confidentiality as a huge issue in the coaching engagement that must be honored consistently. They state, "The coach has the duty to respect the confidentiality of the executive's information, and must refrain from disclosing it even to the party compensating him, except as otherwise waived or agreed by the executive, or as required by law" (p. 362). Morgan, Harkins, & Goldsmith (2005) similarly view confidentiality as important, no matter who is paying the bill. To create an effective coaching relationship, the coachee must feel comfortable openly discussing situations, feelings, concerns, and attitudes that may include individuals of all levels that the coachee works with.

Whitworth, Kimsey-House, and Sandahl (2010) point out that from a confidentiality perspective, the coach cannot guarantee an a priori agreement. They argue that there may be circumstances that may cause the coach to reveal confidentiality to a higher authority, such as someone in the legal profession. They state that it is important for coaches to inform their coachees that their confidence is not privileged under the law and also that a coach may be subpoenaed for information.

Trust is an integral characteristic of a coaching partnership that must be earned so that the coach may provide the right balance of challenges and support for the coachee throughout the engagement (Peterson, 1996). Trust in the coaching relationship is what allows the coachee to truly be open to and influenced by the coaching (Kiel, Rimmer, Williams, & Doyle, 1996).

However, building trust is not a cookie-cutter process. As Ting and Scisco (2015) state, "Trust looks differently behaviorally to [different people]" (p. 37). Therefore, the coach must consistently work on building and facilitating trust including "constant awareness and monitoring of [the client's] behaviors and motivations that may bear on how his or her trustworthiness is perceived by others, and an understanding and respect for what trust means to the person being coached" (Ting & Scisco, 2015, p. 37). Trust is so crucial to the relationship that little success can be achieved without it. One way to build trust is to honor confidentiality (Morgan et al., 2005). Candid dialogue can "serve as a powerful relationship-builder and as a model of the kind of frank discussions that form the foundation of any worthwhile coaching relationship" (Morgan et al., 2005, p. 5).

Figure 4.1 gives an example of a coaching conversation process and gives a good picture of what a "typical" coaching conversation can look like. However, the literature and research help to create some additional ideas about the most important components of a coaching process. Based on all of the research, the coaching process can be broken down into a few categories.

Contracting and Reaching an Agreement

The first step in any coaching engagement is the contracting of the relationship and the coaching engagement itself. This includes discussing payment, frequency of meeting, and the modality of the meeting. It also includes designing the overarching focus of the entire coaching engagement.

Asking Powerful Questions

Coaching is all about asking as opposed to telling. After reaching an agreement, the coach works with the client to uncover where he or she would like to start and what he or she would like to focus on. This is largely accomplished through the use of powerful questions. The true power of coaching

---

General Coaching Conversation Example

Rapport Building
The coach and the client connect and take a moment to say hello and possibly check in on how the client is doing since their last opportunity to speak. This set up of the conversation can set the tone for support and trust.

Agenda Creation and Goal Setting
In this section, the coach will support and partner with the client to identify the topic for the coaching conversation, what outcomes the client would like to achieve and possibly other goals for the discussion.

Exploration
This is the part of the coaching conversation where the coach and the client explore what is important about the goal and look deeply at where they are now in relation to where they would like to be or what they would like to achieve.

Gathering and Selecting Options
Once the client has explored the current state and addressed the gap between the current state and the desired future state or goal, the coach and the client partner explore options to move towards the goal.

Committing to Action
In this part, the coach partners with the client to assess and encourage commitment to a step or steps towards reaching the client's goal.

Wrapping Up and Reflection
The final stage is a review of the coaching session, with an opportunity for the client to reflect on their learning and give any feedback to the coach.

Figure 4.1   Coaching conversation example.

comes from the power of questions. As a new coach, it is often difficult to stay in pure, question focused coaching mode and stay away from the tendency to give advice. With practice this becomes easier, but it does take practice. There are four main types of questions.

Open Questions

Questions such as "What does it look like to do a better job?" or "What is important to you about being a better leader?" are open questions. Open questions are the most powerful questions that a coach can ask. Open questions intentionally invite the client to give longer and more robust answers that can contribute to a greater amount of discovery and awareness.

Closed Questions

Questions such as, "Can you speak Spanish?" or "How many times a week to you exercise?" are closed questions. Closed questions, in the simplest sense, are questions that can be answered with a single word such as a yes or a no. Since closed questions can be answered with a single word, they have less power than open questions that give the client the space to process his or her thoughts and ideas.

Leading Questions

Leading questions are often suggestions that are hidden in the form of a question. Some examples are:

- Do you think you should come up with a new plan to move forward?
- Have you sought out advice from someone who has already done this?
- What types of training might you consider to get better at this?
- Would it be helpful if you spoke to your boss about the changes that you want to make?

As you can see, these examples are questions in the most basic sense, however, the problem is that they may be guiding the listener to think in a specific way or to think of a specific solution. While giving advice is not part of coaching in its purest form, by definition, asking for permission to step out of the coaching process to offer advice would be preferable over asking leading questions.

Multiple-Part Questions

Multipart questions are a series of questions that are often asked in rapid succession. When questions are quickly asked one after the other it is difficult for the client to have an opportunity to answer all of them. Therefore, even if each part of the multipart question is powerful, the question overall, will lose some of its power because it was compounded. For example: "What is the best way to coach this team? I mean, should we start by coaching the leaders and then coaching the rest of the team, or should we just get everyone started at the same time? What would be a good way to think about this?" While questions like this might be common and acceptable in our everyday conversation, they are not very helpful in the coaching process.

Powerful questioning could also be called thought-provoking questioning. The power from a question truly comes from the question's ability to generate awareness and inspire a broader range of thought. When asking coaching questions, tap into your genuine curiosity. Be open to whatever the answer may be. If we are asking questions that we already know the answer to, we are lessening the power of the question.

Generating Awareness

Another important part of the coaching process is generating awareness. Generating awareness involves helping the client uncover his or her own ideas, thoughts, and feelings that help the client move toward his or her desired outcomes and goals. The International Coach Federation (ICF) has given some definition to what awareness in coaching looks like.

- Goes beyond what is said by assessing client's concerns and not getting hooked by the client's descriptions of their experience.
- Invokes inquiry for greater understanding, awareness, and clarity.
- Identifies for the client his or her underlying concerns; typical and fixed ways of perceiving himself or herself and the world; differences between the facts and the interpretation; and disparities between thoughts, feelings, and action.
- Helps clients to discover for themselves the new thoughts, beliefs, perceptions, emotions, moods, and so on, that strengthen their ability to take action and achieve what is important to them.
- Communicates broader perspectives to clients and inspires commitment to shift their viewpoints and find new possibilities for action.
- Helps clients to see the different, interrelated factors that affect them and their behaviors (e.g., thoughts, emotions, body, and background).
- Expresses insights to clients in ways that are useful and meaningful for the client.
- Identifies major strengths vs. major areas for learning and growth and what is most important to address during coaching.
- Asks the client to distinguish between trivial and significant issues, situational vs. recurring behaviors, when detecting a separation between what is being stated and what is being done.

An additional technique to help the client gain awareness is through paraphrasing and summarizing what the client is saying. When a coach reflects back to the client his or her own language, thought processes, and ideas, it can help the client gain greater awareness and clarity about what is getting in his or her way and how to move past it. It also gives the coach the opportunity to "check in" and make sure he or she is understanding the client correctly.

Setting Goals

Coaching conversations are most always goal focused. The coach partners with the coachee to not only identify a topic, but to co-create a goal that will be the focus of the coaching. Often, the coaching engagement itself has a larger, overarching agreement and focus for the whole of the coaching partnership. Goal setting is also done based on a specific agreement within each individual coaching session.

Measuring Success

One of the largest challenges for coaching practitioners is to represent and articulate the value of coaching. Most coaching clients will tell you that they find value in the coaching process. However, they are often not able to put a specific metric of measurement on that value. Let's take a look at a few different ways that coaching success can be measured.

Measuring Return on Investment (ROI)

In the business world, ROI, is the main way that success is measured. As most coaching practitioners will tell you, this can be a challenge. It is a challenge because often times, the benefits of coaching are obvious to the client's but seem to be less obvious to the accounting department. O'Neill (2007) suggests that the best solution is to involve the client in the analysis and evaluation of the bottom-line benefits of coaching. This can specifically be done by working with the client to identify three specific factors that they want to improve.

1. Customize those three factors until they are specific and measure-able.
2. Partner with the client to identify additional variables that will impact the results.
3. Check in often on the progress during the coaching engagement.
4. Evaluate the success by identifying the final business results in a measurable way (dollars, percentages, etc.).

Measuring Well-Being

Grant (Grant & Spence, 2010) contends that financial ROI can be considered a somewhat unreliable measure of organizational coaching outcome. Instead, he recommends looking at two additional important variables for coaching in organizational settings. These are well-being and workplace engagement. Organizations function better with productive employees who are engaged in their work activities, and these should be some of the key metrics in evaluating coaching success. These humanistic metrics are able to give a far more meaningful and holistic view of the impact of a coaching intervention than any financial figure.

The well-being and engagement framework was created by Grant and Spence (2010) as a more holistic way to measure coaching success through assessing the client's well-being (Figure 4.2). It measures the dimensions of well-being and workplace engagement.

Measuring Return on Expectations

A newer perspective on measuring coaching success is taking a look at the return on expectations. This is a measure that is becoming increasingly popular in the training and development field.

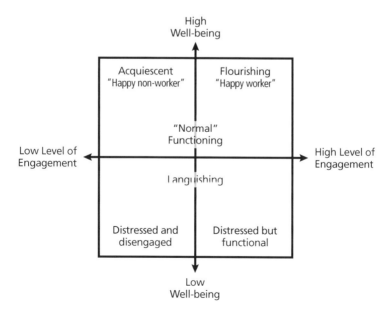

Figure 4.2   Return on expectations. *Source:* Grant and Spence (2010).

Don Kirkpatrick (1959) presented his thoughts about training evaluation in a series of articles published in the *American Society for Training and Development Journal*. He presented what is known today as the Kirkpatrick four level evaluation model: reaction, learning, behavior, and results. In his book, *Implementing the Four Levels*, Don and his son Jim (Kirkpatrick & Kirkpatrick, 2007) discussed the "importance of evaluating the four levels, or as many as you can, in sequence" to "build a compelling chain of evidence as to the value of learning to the bottom line" (p. 123). They emphasized the need to present the value of training in a way that will "maximize the meaningfulness to the hearts and minds of your internal stakeholders" (Kirkpatrick & Kirkpatrick, 2007, p. 123).

Over recent years, Kirkpatrick's original work has evolved. Kirkpatrick's daughter-in-law later expanded his original work by creating the new world four levels and the Kirkpatrick business partnership model. This model emphasizes the process of working with clients and organizational coaching sponsors to accomplish return on stakeholder expectations. Kirkpatrick and Kirkpatrick (2007) describe return on expectations as the best indicator of value. It is a more comprehensive and holistic measurement of benefits of training (Kirkpatrick & Kirkpatrick, 2009).

Although this concept has evolved out of measuring training effectiveness, it is very relevant for coaching. To achieve return on expectations, coaches must ask questions to clarify and refine the expectations of key business stakeholders as they attempt to satisfy the stakeholders and convert their expectations into observable, measurable business, or mission outcomes. Because a great deal of employee learning occurs on the job, the Kirkpatricks emphasize the need for learning professionals to also partner with supervisors and managers to encourage them to prepare participants for training or coaching and to play a key role after training by reinforcing newly learned knowledge and skills through support and accountability.

Chapter Summary

Although one of the tenets of coaching is to meet the client where he or she is at and to allow a high degree of flexibility that allows for the client to set the tone and direction of the coaching, it is important to allow the process of coaching to create a structure or framework for coaching sessions that align the coaching goals with the overall coaching agreement and give the client and the coach a process to lean on that will support them in the coaching.

As coaching can be a significant investment, it is also important to understand how the success of coaching can be measured and represented both for clients as well as sponsoring organizations when applicable. There is no one "right" way to measure coaching success but there are many ways that the value of coaching can be expressed.

Chapter Reflection Questions

1. How do the ICF 11 Core Competencies inform the coaching process when working with clients?
2. What do you feel are the best metrics for coaching success?
3. How can those metrics be explained to the sponsors and/or recipients of coaching?

Activities

1. Without telling others what you are doing, practice asking only open-ended questions for an entire day. It is harder than you think! Make note in the change of the dynamic of your conversations as you switch to this type of questioning. What do you notice? How are your conversations becoming more robust or more powerful?
2. Without telling others what you are doing, practice not giving any advice for an entire day. Instead, ask questions. For example, if someone asks you, "What do you think?," instead of giving a suggestion or a statement, ask them a question such as, "What do you feel?" or "What do you think?"

References

Axmith, M. (2004). Executive coaching: A catalyst for personal growth and corporate change. *Ivey Business Journal*, May/June, 1–5.

Diedrich, R. C. (1996). An iterative approach to executive coaching. *Consulting Psychology Journal: Practice and Research, 48*(2), 61–66.

Grant, A. M., & Spence, G. B. (2010). Using coaching and positive psychology to promote a flourishing workforce: A model of goal-striving and mental health. In P. A. Linley, S. Harrington, & N. Page (Eds.), *Oxford handbook of positive psychology and work* (pp. 175–188). Oxford, England: Oxford University Press.

Johnson, H. (2002). A brand new you. *Training, 39*(8), 14.

Johnson, L. K. (2007). Getting more from executive coaching. *Harvard Management Update, January*, 3–6.

Kiel, F., Rimmer, E., Williams, K., & Doyle, M. (1996). Coaching at the top. *Consulting Psychology Journal: Practice and Research, 48*(2), 67–77.

Kilburg, R. R. (1996). Toward a conceptual understanding and definition of executive coaching. *Consulting Psychology Journal: Practice and Research, 48*(2), 134–144.

Kirkpatrick, D. L., & Kirkpatrick, J. D. (2007). *Implementing the four levels: A practical guide for effective evaluation of training programs.* San Francisco, CA: Berrett-Koehler.

Kirkpatrick, J., & Kirkpatrick, W. K. (2009, April). *The Kirkpatrick Four Levels: A Fresh Look after 50 Years 1959–2009.* Retrieved from http://www.kirkpatrickpartners.com/Portals/0/Resources/Kirkpatrick%20Four%20Levels%20white%20paper.pdf

Morgan, H., Harkins, P., & Goldsmith, M. (Eds.). (2005). *The art and practice of leadership coaching: 50 top executive coaches reveal their secrets.* Hoboken, NJ: Wiley and Sons.

Natale, S. M., & Diamante, T. (2005). The five stages of executive coaching: Better process makes better practice. *Journal of Business Ethics, 59,* 361–374.

O'Neill, M. (2007). *Executive coaching with backbone and heart* (2nd ed). San Francisco, CA: Jossey-Bass.

Peterson, D. B. (1996). Executive coaching at work: The art of one-on-one change. *Consulting Psychology Journal: Practice and Research, 48*(2), 78–86.

Ting, S., & Scisco, P. (2015). *The CCL handbook of coaching: A guide for the leader coach.* San Francisco, CA: Jossey-Bass.

Weinberger, J. (1995). Common factors aren't so common: The common factors dilemma. *Clinical Psychology: Science and Practice, 2*(1), 45–69.

Whitworth, L., Kimsey-House, H., & Sandahl, P. (2010). *Co-active coaching: New skills for coaching people toward success in work and life.* Palo Alto, CA: Davies-Black.

5

The Role of the Coach

The role of the coach is to help the client achieve objectives through facilitated deep learning and sustained change while providing continuous feedback and support (King & Eaton, 1999; Zweibel, 2005). A coach facilitates this by helping "the [client] maintain a consistent, confident focus on tuning up strengths and managing shortcomings" (Tobias, 1996, p. 87). This continuous learning, support, encouragement, and feedback offered by the coach help the executive to challenge his or her own potential and to confront resistance. Through the coaching process, and as new insights arise for the executive, the coach helps the executive prioritize goals along with an action plan for development and behavior change (Peterson, 1996). Coaches must be well trained in the coaching process, skills, and competencies. Credentialing should also be strongly considered by all coaching practitioners to help uphold the validity of the profession.

The Role of a Coach

The role of the coach is to be in full support of the client in alignment with his or her goals and objectives. In essence, the coach's role is to be a catalyst

An Introduction to Professional and Executive Coaching, pages 67–82
Copyright © 2018 by Information Age Publishing
67

for change by helping the client to acquire new skills and knowledge, thus sparking learning and growth. Throughout the process the coaching approach is tailored specifically to the needs of that client (Evered & Selman, 1989). Similarly, Peterson (1996) explains, "The role of the coach is to find the best way for an individual to learn a specific skill" (p. 80). Ting and Scisco (2015) suggest how this objective might be attained: "Good coaches know how to listen, find core values, empathize, reflect, probe, ask questions, relate issues, challenge, foster alternative scenario, find network resources, foster alliances, sustain ongoing evaluation, and conduct strategic reviews" (p. 17).

Skills that coaches use include building and sustaining rapport, listening effectively, reading nonverbal behavior, asking powerful questions, reframing, setting goals, and eliciting commitment (King & Eaton, 1999; Whitworth, Kimsey-House, & Sandahl, 2010). As supported by several studies, skillful, powerful questioning by the coach is at the core of the coaching relationship, as it propels forward movement in the client and is, therefore, essential to effective coaching (Turner, 2006; Whitworth et al., 2010). The art of questioning provokes new insights within a client and the discovery of answers by the client (Richard, 2003; Zweibel, 2005). Getting to the truth of the matter by asking provocative questions is necessary in order to get to the real issues. Whitworth et al. (2010) distinguish what they deem as powerful questioning from regular questions. They state that asking open-ended, powerful questions send a client on an inner journey, inviting introspection and generating meaningful insights (Whitworth et al., 2010). In summary, "an effective coach must have the skill, stamina, and wherewithal to ask continually stimulating questions that challenge the executive's thinking and judgment in order to spark new perspectives on problem solving and solutions" (Axmith, 2004, p. 17).

Additional skills that a coach employs during a coaching session include interpersonal effectiveness, good listening, empathy, patience, flexibility, analytical problem solving, creativity, and humor (Wasylyshyn, 2003). Moreover, the Corporate Leadership Council (CLC, 2005) identified mediating between the executive and his or her colleagues, assessing an executive's strengths and weaknesses, clarifying issues, reviewing progress, and educating the executive on management and interpersonal skills. Effectively giving feedback is another important skill for a coach to possess (Diedrich, 1996; O'Neil, 2007). Diedrich (1996) says that an effective coach employs specificity, empathy, and inquiry when providing feedback to a client. According to Diedrich (1996), in order to be effective, feedback should be empathetic, detailed in that it refers to actual behavior, and open-ended. Kilburg (1996) contends that feedback is a major key to success. Ting and

Scisco (2015) state that "a characteristic of coaching is that coaches are guided by the values they possess, along with the values of their client, although this is not a skill. By accessing these values, as well as the emotional and mental vitality of their clients, coaches spark transformative directions and goals of the client" (p. 29). According to them, coaches ask deep-level questions to get to a client's purpose, as well as the values that guide his or her passions.

Whitworth et al. (2010) state that a client can make decisions that are more successful when the client understands his or her values and makes decisions that align with those values. Whitworth et al. (2010) add that living in one's values fully may not be easy and can be uncomfortable at first, however, once this discomfort passes, the client is able to pursue a more fulfilling life. Indeed, Whitworth et al. (2010) claim that coaches who do not live within their values will experience an ungratifying life rather than fulfillment.

The effectiveness of the relationship is strongly based on the coach's view of the client. King and Eaton (1999) say, "A good coach must believe unequivocally in the potential of the [client] and operate on the assumption that the [client] is the real expert about themselves and their work" (p. 146). Wright (2005) similarly states that it is important that coaches view clients as "well and whole . . . rather than as needing to be fixed" (p. 326). Wright (2005) asserts that success increases when people become empowered and are aware of their capabilities. Levinson (1996) emphasizes that the term *coach* should be taken seriously, as this is a shared relationship between peers. The concept of a shared peer relationship is also advocated by Wright (2005). These authors agree that the coach and the client are equal contributors to the success of the relationship. All of these skills play an important part in determining the role of a coach. However, the role of the coach also includes the ethical responsibility of proper training, coaching credentialing, and supervision. Next, we will take a look at each of these important aspects of the coaching role.

Coach Training and Coaching Credentials

The background and credentials of coaches are like mosaic tiles in that each coach's breadth, depth, and type of experience is unique. Today one sees people hanging their "coaching shingle" without actually possessing qualified training or credentials. This challenges the integrity of the profession and needs to be addressed. With the immense growth of the coaching profession, training, and credentialing have become paramount.

The criteria of common credentials for executive coaches include "having an understanding of psychological dynamics, adult development and learning, business management, leadership, and political issues" (Kampa-Kokesch & Anderson, 2010, p. 221).

The number of coach training programs that have been created over the last few decades has increased dramatically, and with this growth there have been challenges with regulations and common standards to measure these programs against. The International Coach Federation (ICF) has been the leading force behind working to create curriculum standards for training. However, many training schools have created their own credentialing system.

There are now more than 60 different credentials in North America and the United Kingdom as well as other countries, and various systems used to grant these credentials. Some of these programs are purely competency based. Others require attaining specific hours of courses and completing projects or course work. Some programs require supervision by someone who has already attained a coaching credential, while some rely on self-assessment or can even be obtained without ever coaching a client. Any coaching credential based simply on self-proclamation is a danger to the credibility of the profession.

With so much variation of different coaching programs and credentials, it is important to gain clarity and reduce the confusion about coaching credentialing. There needs to be greater education and guidance provided to prospective coaches, current coaches, and the general public about the nature of, sources for, and issues associated with coaching credentials.

There is also some confusion regarding various terms associated with credentials in coaching, specifically the difference between the terms credential and certification. The term *credential* (not certification) is the more accurate and all encompassing. This more general category of credentialing includes other terms such as *certification, accreditation, licensure,* and *registration,* as well as the terms typically associated with universities such as *diploma* and *degree.* For coaching, the primary focus is on certification and accreditation since these are the most popular form of credentialing in coaching.

Perspectives on Certification for Coaches

Carr (2015) conducted a comprehensive study to look at the various coaching credentials. One of the aspects of his study was to look at the different perspectives that practicing coaches have about coaching credentials. There were several perspectives on the importance of certification for coaches that arose from the coaches that participated in his study. Below is the summary of his findings:

- Certification is a political tool.
- Certification is arbitrary.
- Certification is a revenue generator.
- Certification is a weak substitute for integrity.
- Certification acts as a mark of distinction.
- Certification protects the public.
- Certification acts as a beacon.

Certification is a Political Tool

Various organizations are in a struggle to control coaching certification. Although the organizations suggest that their emphasis on certification is primarily to benefit the coaching industry, the general public (and potential clients), and coaches themselves; critics respond by saying that the primary beneficiary of certification is the organization (through fees collected for either membership, certification processing, or certification procedures; Carr, 2015).

Certification is Arbitrary

Certification based on hours of experience may be a way to underscore the importance of experience, but hour-based approaches are at best arbitrary and at worst misleading the public. Is a coach with 250 hours of experience really less able than a coach with 500 hours of experience? It might be logical to say, "yes," but there is too little evidence that such hour designations are equivalent to capability. In reality, the use of hours to determine certification is probably based on the standard university system of awarding a degree after completion of a certain number of units or courses (Carr, 2015).

Certification is a Revenue Generator

Of all the negative views expressed about certification this one is the most prevalent. Considerable cynicism appears to exist regarding the "real" reason versus the "stated" reason for certification. However, while it may generate revenue (or income) in that there is typically a fee associated with it, certification is not likely to be a "profit" generator. Instead, it is more likely to be a costly and time-consuming procedure that is offered as a service rather than a "profit-center." To be conducted with even minimal credibility, coaching schools and associations are required to engage in considerable review, paperwork, and communication (Carr, 2015).

Certification is a Weak Substitute for Integrity

Many experienced coaches believe that certification is unnecessary. This is partly based on the idea that their actions are more important than their certificates. Actions typically include their attention to training themselves to offer the best possible quality of service, ethics, integrity, and skills to assist clients. In addition, many coaches believe that the results their clients have gained or the outcomes their clients have achieved ought to be the main qualification (Carr, 2015).

Certification Acts as a Mark of Distinction

The most popular view for certification is that it distinguishes "charlatans" and the unskilled (and unscrupulous) from qualified, trained, and skilled coaches. Coaches who hold this view also hope that such certification will attract more prospective clients and act as a shorthand way for coaches to demonstrate their capability. While it seems logical that a coach engaged in serious, systematic study and supervised practice will be more likely to attract clients than someone who has no formal training in coaching, too little data is available to assess the validity of this viewpoint (Carr, 2015).

Certification Protects the Public

This is a common viewpoint that supports certification systems used in many other disciplines. Currently, the ICF does have a process in place to provide scrutiny or discipline for certified members that engage in inappropriate, illegal, or immoral activities (Carr, 2015).

Certification Acts as a Beacon

Many supporters of certification acknowledge its weaknesses, but believe that it is a way to improve the quality of coaching, document a coach's training, and provide an opportunity for coaching schools to validate the progress of their participants. Advocates believe that certification is more of a starting point than an end in itself. Proponents of certification believe there is a positive movement among various coach training schools to tailor their offerings to conform to the certification requirements of a particular coaching association. They see this movement toward commonality as a way to establish more widely accepted standards and provide greater opportunities for industry self-regulation (Carr, 2015).

Three of these themes from the study can be considered positive or supportive of certification, whereas the others could be considered critical of certification. Although there are a number of concerns raised about the value of credentialing, the process of creating consistency and regulation of the coaching profession is important in order to uphold its integrity and the professionalization of the coaching field (Carr, 2015).

Categories Used to Determine and Define Coaching Credentials

In order to clarify and distinguish between the variety of credentialing systems available to coaches and potential coaches, Carr (2015) created a review of all known forms of certification, registration, diplomas, and degree granting in coaching. This study outlined the relevant categories used to determine and define the various types of coaching credentials. The categories are listed below:

- initials of credential,
- full title of credential,
- issuing source of credential,
- training hours required to obtain credential,
- coaching hours required to obtain credential,
- paper/essay required to obtain credential,
- examination required to obtain credential, and
- membership required to obtain or maintain credential.

Initials

The use of this shortcut for describing the type of credential has led to extensive confusion as to what the letters actually mean. Many coaches place these initials after their names on business cards, websites, or other forms of interaction with clients and the public. Unlike the more well-known initials such as MD or PhD, the proliferation of the initials in the coaching world has decreased the likelihood of public recognition. Some initials from different organizations may consist of identical letters, but represent different words in the full title. A few sets of initials are identical in letters and title, but are offered by different organizations (Carr, 2015).

Full Title

The most frequently used form of credentialing in coaching is certification. Consequently, most titles include the term certification. Some schools use the term certificate, diploma, or registered. While these terms are not synonymous, they do share some common elements. Typically, they all reflect that a person has participated in some type of systematic, predetermined course of study and practice and has been awarded the designation as a result of the successful completion of specific requirements. However, those requirements can range from attendance only to passing examinations to writing extensive documents to demonstrating specific skills or abilities to graduating from an accredited school. Typically, certification (as distinct from a diploma, degree, or registration) means additional post-certification requirements such as continuing education or other activities that contribute to quality assurance. While certification does not guarantee competence, it is strongly oriented in that direction and usually includes some type of eligibility requirements (often prior to admission to either the training program or the professional field) as well as an evaluation of each person's skills and knowledge (Carr, 2015).

Issuing Source

The credentialing issuer is the school, association, or organization responsible for creating or conferring the particular title. There are six sources of credentialing:

1. coaching schools that tailor (or align) their curriculum so that participants will be eligible for certification by the ICF;
2. coaching schools that offer their own in-house certification (or combine their in-house certification with [1] above);
3. coaching associations that provide certification such as the ICF and the International Association of Coaches;
4. coaching associations that sponsor particular training programs such as the Worldwide Association of Business Coaches;
5. universities that offer master's degrees or doctoral degrees, or certificates and diplomas that emphasize coaching; and
6. individuals who "self-proclaim" their own certification.

Accredited

Accreditation, which is not the same as certification, has been used extensively around the world for determining the quality and legitimacy of postsecondary educational organizations. Independent bodies have been formed in various countries to review colleges and universities and assign or deny accredited status. In North America, college and university accrediting is carried out by regional, (as compared to national), independent groups. Professional associations in North America also review specific offerings at colleges and universities and determine whether such a specialized program qualifies for their accreditation. Traditional examples in North America include law schools, medical schools, and advanced degree programs in psychology, counseling, and social work. In Europe, it is more likely that the terms accreditation and certification are used interchangeably. In North America, the term accredited is more properly applied only to organizations and not individuals (Carr, 2015).

In coaching, there are three associations currently involved in accrediting coaching schools: the ICF, the International Institute of Coaching and Mentoring (IICM), and the Open Learning Institute (OLI). The IICM and the OLI are both located in the United Kingdom. Unlike the traditional university accrediting sources in the United States, these bodies do not possess the "arms-length," independent relationship between themselves and the schools they are accrediting. They do, however, in the case of the ICF, for example, provide explicit criteria and standards upon which their accrediting decisions are made.

Many of these accredited programs have geared their curriculum to match the requirements for certification with the ICF. Schools typically call this "alignment" and it means that the courses, contact hours, and experiences required to obtain their credential will enable individuals to apply for one of the three certifications (ACC, PCC, MCC) provided by the ICF. The ICF has provided a portfolio method whereby applicants from schools the ICF does not currently accredit can independently apply for certification (Carr, 2015).

Training Hours

Another common requirement is the number of hours of coach training that a coach receives. In some cases, the organization distinguishes between direct contact hours (typically contact with a course leader either in-person or through telecourse) and indirect hours (typically study time required, time to complete assignments, or time engaging in research or practice projects; Carr, 2015).

Coaching Hours

Coaching hours are a common requirement of many coaching training programs and credentialing organizations. Typically, this number represents the minimum number of hours of coaching with paid or unpaid clients (as compared to "coaching" fellow students in the class through simulations or role plays) in order to gain the noted credential. In some cases, organizations do not require a minimum number of hours and instead require a minimum number of clients (rather than hours) and a minimum number of sessions with each client (Carr, 2015).

Paper/Essay

Many coaching schools provide instruction via telecourse and few require written assignments. Often, coaching schools require written work that is typically a case study, journal, or position paper. The emphasis here is on written work that must be reviewed by or turned into school faculty (Carr, 2015).

Examination

Oral or/and written examinations are common and typically occur near or at the end of coursework and coaching hours. In some cases, these exams are conducted on an interim basis. Programs leading to traditional degrees such as an MA or PhD more typically require a dissertation or thesis (Carr, 2015).

Membership Required

A very small number of credentials require that the holder be a member in good standing (fees paid) of a particular organization or association.

Although there is arguably value in most of the coach training and credentialing offerings available, as discussed in Chapter 2, there are also set standards that contribute to what is considered a profession. Bennet (2006) defines criteria for a profession. Some of these include:

- minimum levels of education and training required to become proficient (accepted competencies and skill sets);
- practice grounded in identified bodies of knowledge and avenues of communication and idea exchange;
- an agreed set of ethical standards by which coaching can self-discipline practice, including avenues of enforcement;
- widely accepted professional organizations that represent the profession and those practicing it;
- systems for evaluating merit or certifying competence that are widely accepted and allow for further development of the profession; and
- external recognition of coaching's professional status by those served and the general public.

There are many coaching specific organizations such as the ICF, the European Mentoring and Coaching Council (EMCC), the Worldwide Association of Business Coaches (WABC), and the International Association of Coaches (IAC). However, as addressed in Chapter 1, the two largest organizations are the ICF and IAC.

Both were founded by the late Thomas J. Leonard, who is often credited as being the founder of today's profession of coaching. Although each of these organizations has its own requirements and frameworks for coaching skills (the ICF has 11 coaching competencies, while the IAC has 9 masteries), both organizations provide ethical frameworks, training opportunities, and certification processes.

Coaches seeking certification go through coaching training programs, log coaching hours with clients and with a mentor coach (ICF), take a written or online exam, submit recorded coaching sessions for review, and pay fees in order to obtain certification.

Both organizations require their certified coaches to maintain their memberships with the ICF or IAC and to renew their credentials either annually (IAC) or every 3 years (ICF). They are also expected to continue to develop their skills through continuing education and additional coach training.

By establishing high professional standards and a strong code of ethics, organizations like the ICF and IAC ensure that the coaches they grant a credential to will offer a high level of knowledge, coaching skills, and integrity. It is a symbol of protection and service for customers; a symbol you want to have next to your name.

Coaching Supervision

One additional aspect of coaching credentialing that upholds the integrity of the profession and inspires excellence in practice is supervision. The ICF (2017) defines *coaching supervision* as the interaction that occurs when a coach periodically brings his or her coaching work experiences to a coaching supervisor in order to engage in reflective dialogue and collaborative learning for the development and benefit of the coach and his or her clients. The process of coaching supervision gives coaches and coach trainees a rich and robust opportunity to reflect on their own coaching and the opportunity to strengthen their own coaching performance. Sometimes the term mentor coaching is used interchangeably with coaching supervision. However, supervision is different from mentor coaching. Mentor coaching is an additional professional development opportunity or activity for coaches. Mentor coaching focuses on expanding and strengthening demonstration of coaching behaviors and coaching skills.

The ICF considers supervision of coaching to be beneficial in two ways: It serves to support the coach's personal development and it also serves to increase the strength of the client experience from coaching. For these reasons, the ICF Global Board has a specific policy on coaching supervision and which activities are eligible to satisfy ICF's credential renewal requirements.

Coaching supervision provides coaches with an opportunity to continually develop their skills as well as providing a quality control element on behalf of their clients. Coaching supervision is important even if your coaching is going well because there is a value to learning from another coaching professional and analyzing what's working and why it's working. It is also a process that helps coaches to identify their coaching strengths. Coaching supervision helps coaches to gain a better understanding of their clients.

Having supervision is a fundamental aspect of continuing personal and professional development for coaches, mentors and consultants. Supervision provides a protected and disciplined space in which the coach can reflect on particular client situations and relationships. Supervision can profoundly benefit the client, the client organization and his or her own professional practice. Despite this, coaching supervision was noticeable by its absence in the first 20 years of the growth of this new profession, but at the turn of the century it began to be advocated by a number of key writers (Downey, 1999; Flaherty, 1999).

In some comprehensive research, Hawkins and Schwenk (2006) explored reasons for the lack of development of coaching supervision. In interview and focus groups with experienced coaches the main reasons were

- lack of clarity about what supervision involves,
- lack of well-trained supervisors,
- lack of commitment to personal development as it makes us vulnerable, and
- lack of discipline among coaches.

This research also explored the following questions:

1. What is coaching supervision?
2. Why should HR professionals be interested in it?
3. What do HR professionals need to know about coaching supervision?
4. What does good practice look like?
5. How can supervision help coaching to be more effective?

The findings were as follows:

- Coaching supervision was much advocated but poorly practiced.
- The strong majority of coaches felt that coaches should have regular ongoing supervision of their coaching.

- Only 44% receive regular ongoing supervision.
- Many of those who were participating in supervisions were consulting with supervisors of counseling or psychotherapy and some with peers without supervision training themselves.
- There was a shortage of training courses for coaching supervision.
- This was the first research in the field of coaching supervision.
- There was an absence of specific models and methodologies for coaching supervision.

In 2013, Hawkins and Smith defined supervision as the process by which a coach with the help of a supervisor can attempt to better understand both the client system and themselves as part of the client–coach system, and by so doing transform his or her work and develop his or her craft (Hawkins & Smith, 2013).

So, what should supervision look like? The 5 stage coaching model CLEAR (contract, listen, explore, action, review) that was discussed in Chapter 3, can actually be applied as a framework for coaching supervision.

CLEAR Model

This model was designed by Peter Hawkins and came from his background in therapy, supervision, and organizational management (see Figure 5.1).

Five Stages

Contracting

Contracting, in essence, is about the questions: "What is our goal?"; "Why are we here?"; "What will we do?"; "Who will do it?"; "How will we do it?"; and "How often?"

Listening

Along with using the appropriate interventions, listening helps the coach to assist the client in putting together a clear and accurate representation of his or her world, his or her goals, and his or her insights.

Figure 5.1   CLEAR model. *Source:* Hawkins & Smith, 2006.

Exploring

Hawkins and Schwenk (2006) use exploring to represent two things: (a) Looking at the impact of the current situation on the client and (b) exploring possibilities to move forward and generate action.

Action

This is working with the client to take forward-moving action toward achieving his or her desired outcomes and goals.

Review

In this stage of the model, the client reviews what has changed for them, what shifts or insights he or she has made and what he or she will do more of or will do differently going forward. Hawkins and Smith (2013) also point out that it is important that supervision not just be seen as an activity carried out by a supervisor who is "above" or "superior" to the coaching being supervised. Instead, it should be viewed as a joint activity done in full partnership, with the goals of ensuring quality of practice, capacity, and capability development and making sure that the coach is resourcing himself or herself effectively for what he or she is undertaking. This can be accomplished by creating a relationship that is co-creative and supportive of generative thinking that allows for new learning to be created and applied for the benefit of the coach, the supervisor, and the profession as a whole.

Tips on Getting the Most From Coaching Supervision

1. Prepare an agenda of what you want to discuss with your supervising coach during your time together to ensure that you are both clear on the goals and objectives.
2. Keep your own notes about the takeaways and topics covered in the coaching supervision session so that you can reflect on these after the session is complete.
3. Ensure that you and your coaching supervisor set regular review dates to consider your coaching supervision relationship, its effectiveness and your development needs, and how these can best be met.

Chapter Summary

The role of coaching encompasses embracing, developing, and leveraging a specific set of skills, however, it also includes important aspects such as coaching training, credentialing, and supervision. These standards and consistent measures will bring the consistency that is needed to quell the perceptions that coaching is an unregulated and rogue profession with little quality control. The ICF, along with a few other coaching organizations have made great strides in standardizing coaching training programs and coaching credentialing. It is important to educate the general public about the importance of coach training and coach credentials.

Chapter Reflection Questions

1. How would you define supervision, who and what it serves, and the value it creates?
2. How would you contract for and build a collaborative partnership between the supervisor and coach being supervised?
3. How would you evaluate the benefits of supervision for the coach's clients?

Activity

Interview a number of different coaches that have attended different training programs/schools. Ask them about the training curriculum and the certification process. What helped them to choose their training program? Have they gained a coaching credential? If so, what did their credentialing process entail?

References

Axmith, M. (2004, May/June). Executive coaching: A catalyst for personal growth and corporate change. *Ivey Business Journal*, 1–5.

Bennett, J. L. (2006). An agenda for coaching related research: A challenge for researchers. *Consulting Psychology Journal: Practice and Research, 58*, 240–249

Carr, R. A. (2015). *A Guide to Coach Credentials*. Retrieved from http://www.peer.ca/credentials05.html#Anchor-Appendix 6296

Diedrich, R. C. (1996). An iterative approach to executive coaching. *Consulting Psychology Journal: Practice and Research, 48*(2), 61–66.

Downey, M. (1999). *Effective coaching*. London, England: Orion.

Evered, R. D., & Selman, J. C. (1989). Coaching and the art of management. *Organizational Dynamics, 18*, 16–32.

Flaherty, J. (1999). *Coaching: Evoking excellence in others*. Woburn, MA: Butterworth-Heinemann.

Hawkins P., & Schwenk, G. (2006). *Coaching supervision*. London, England: Chartered Institute of Personnel and Development Change Agenda.

Hawkins, P., & Smith N. (2013). *Coaching, mentoring, and organizational consultancy: Supervision and development* (2nd ed.). Maidenhead, England: McGraw-Hill/Open University Press.

International Coach Federation. (2017). *How is coaching distinct from other service professions?* Retrieved June 25, 2017 from https://coachfederation.org/faqs

Kampa-Kokesch, S., & Anderson, M. Z. (2010). Executive coaching: A comprehensive review of literature. *Consulting Psychology Journal: Practice and Research, 53*(4), 205–228.

Kilburg, R. R. (1996). Toward a conceptual understanding and definition of executive coaching. *Consulting Psychology Journal: Practice and Research, 48*(2), 134–144.

King, P., & Eaton, J. (1999). Coaching for results. *Industrial and Commercial Training, 31*(4), 145–148.

Levinson, H. (1996). Executive coaching. *Consulting Psychology Journal: Practice and Research, 48*(2), 115–123.

O'Neil, M. B. (2007). *Executive coaching with backbone and heart: A systems approach to engaging leaders with their challenges.* San Francisco, CA: Jossey-Bass.

Peterson, D. B. (1996). Executive coaching at work: The art of one-on-one change. *Consulting Psychology Journal: Practice and Research, 48*(2), 78–86.

Richard, J. T. (2003). Ideas on fostering creative problem solving in executive coaching. *Consulting Psychology Journal: Practice and Research, 55*(4), 249–256.

Ting, S., & Scisco, P. (2015). *The CCL handbook of coaching: A guide for the leader coach.* San Francisco, CA: Jossey-Bass.

Tobias, L. L. (1996). Coaching executives. *Consulting Psychology Journal: Practice and Research, 48*(2), 87–95.

Turner, C. (2006, May/June). Ungagged: Executives on executive coaching. *Ivey Business Journal,* 1–5.

Wasylyshyn, K. M. (2003). Executive coaching: An outcome study. *Consulting Psychology Journal: Practice and Research, 55*(2), 94–106.

Whitworth, L., Kimsey-House, H., & Sandahl, P. (2010). *Co-active coaching: New skills for coaching people toward success in work and life.* Palo Alto, CA: Davies-Black.

Wright, J. (2005). Workplace coaching: What's it all about? *Work, 24*(3), 325–328.

Zweibel, B. (2005). A strategic coach. *Training and Development, 59*(4), 62–64.

6

Effective Coaching Skills

In Chapter 1 we discussed the International Coach Federation (ICF) coaching competencies. Practicing and embodying the ICF core competencies is important for any coach. However, additional skills have surfaced that contribute to an effective coaching engagement. There are also characteristics and skills that are important for the client to possess.

Criteria Sought When Selecting a Professional Coach

The Corporate Leadership Council (CLC, 2017) reports that organizations highly value a coach's prior experience with coaching professionals, along with training in organizational, industrial psychology or a related field. More specifically, the CLC reports that the skills most sought when selecting a professional coach include the following: strong coaching experience (90% of respondents), degree in psychology or related field (55% of respondents), coaching qualifications or certifications (52% of respondents), experience working as part of a team (27% of respondents), experience working in a line-management position (19% of respondents), experience

An Introduction to Professional and Executive Coaching, pages 83–94
Copyright © 2018 by Information Age Publishing
83

running a business (16% of respondents), and experience working in the industry similar to the client's organization (6% of respondents).

In another report, findings of 87 professionals who have had a coach, report the following sought-after credentials and experience criteria when selecting a coach: 82% reported a preference that their coach had completed graduate studies in psychology or a related field, 78% reported a preference that their coach had experience in or understanding of business, and 25% reported a preference that their coach had an established reputation as a coach (Wasylyshyn, 2003).

As discussed in previous chapters there are a number of coaching credentialing organizations. Currently the International Association of Coaching (IAC) and the ICF are the two most highly acknowledged providers of globally recognized, independent credentialing programs which have existed for more than a decade. "More than 21,000 coaches currently hold one of three offered ICF Credentials" (International Coach Federation, 2017, para. 2). As the ICF (2017) explains, ICF credentials are highly recognized coaching qualifications with credibility around the world. Those consultants who wish to build or maintain a coaching business and wish to be associated with an established group should consider gaining a reputable credential. The mission of the ICF credentialing program includes protecting and serving consumers of coaching services; measuring and certifying competence of individuals, and inspiring pursuit of continuous development.

Currently the ICF has three levels: associate certified coach, professional certified coach, and master certified coach. Each credential requires a specific set of required hours of coach-specific training and coaching experience. The program establishes and administers minimum standards for credentialing professional coaches and coach training agencies, assures the public that participating coaches and coach training agencies meet or exceed these minimum standards, and reinforces professional coaching as a distinct and self-regulating profession.

Credentialing can enhance one's credibility in several ways: it "reassures potential clients that you are an experienced and professional coach, demonstrates that you have high professional standards, demonstrates that you stand by a strong code of ethics, demonstrates a high knowledge and skill level, demonstrates that you take on-going professional development seriously, develops you as a professional coach to further enhance your skills, brings personal satisfaction in achieving a career goal, and reinforces the integrity of the coaching profession internationally" (International Coach Federation, 2017). It is evident that credentialing benefits the coaching by establishing a well-respected standard for credibility.

Coach-Centric Contexts

Aside from the standards of the ICF, professional coaching continues to be unregulated regarding the qualifications of a professional coach (Brotman, Liberi, & Wasylyshyn, 1998; Judge & Cowell, 1997). Indeed, as Grant (2007) asserts, there are currently no generally accepted, identifiable, and distinct skills for coaches. Instead, the practitioner literature has emphasized, from the coach's perspective, skills and characteristics that coaches need in order to be most effective. Moreover, one finds a healthy debate in the literature among practicing professional coaches and researchers as to who is most qualified to be a professional coach (Brotman et al., 1998; Kampa-Kokesch & Anderson, 2010; Kilburg, 1996; Levinson, 1996; Saporito, 1996; Sperry, 1993; Tobias, 1996). Next, we will explore the coaching skills and characteristics that have evolved through the research.

Coach Skills and Characteristics

The following represents the most commonly found coach-centric skills and characteristics that lead to effective professional coaching experiences, as evident in the research.

1. Coaches the whole client and pays attention to the interaction between the client's professional and personal life.
2. Challenges the client to think about new ideas and perspectives.
3. Holds the client accountable for doing the work. Insists that the client take action and create results.
4. Takes a multifaceted approach toward assessing the client's developmental needs, using relevant assessments, observations, and interviews from stakeholders (boss, peers, team members, direct reports) that are critical to the client's development.
5. Delivers immediate competency and action-oriented feedback on the client's developmental goals and progress.
6. Is nonjudgmental, caring, and supportive of the client's situation and needs.
7. Makes the client feel safe and can enable the client to trust the coach with issues of confidentiality.
8. Understands the client's pressures, challenges, responsibilities, and industry in which they work and designs the coaching experience with all of this in mind.
9. Engages immediately and quickly identifies core developmental issues. Helps the client understand the gap between their intention and the impact that they have on others.

10. Listens more than they talk.
11. Asks relevant, probing questions and gets the client to process his or her thoughts and ideas.
12. Grounds the coaching experience around the client's developmental agenda and goals.
13. Motivates the client by recognizing his or her accomplishments when he or she loses focus or becomes discouraged.
14. Brings the client back to the reason for the coaching and intended outcomes, benefits.
15. Stays aware of and does not allow his or her own style, preferences, and feelings to influence the coaching process.
16. Models the behaviors and competencies that the client needs to develop.
17. Provides the client with practical ideas and strategies that he or she can put into action.
18. Remains knowledgeable, up-to-date, and appropriately uses varying activities, exercises, tools, and conceptual models and theories to help the client develop.
19. Helps the client to identify and set clear developmental objectives, goals, and assignments.
20. Is dependable and follows through on what was promised.
21. Understands business, organizations, economic concepts, and issues of management and leadership.
22. Is responsive, readily available, and follows through on what is promised. Flexes to meet the client's changing context and goals.
23. Has a wide range of educational and coaching experience in different industries and in working with professionals across varying developmental career paths.
24. Consistently shows up to the client's coaching sessions with a positive, optimistic, and friendly attitude.

(Brotman et al., 1998; Diedrich & Kilburg, 2001; Kampa-Kokesch & Anderson, 2010; Kilburg, 1996; Levinson, 1996; Saporito, 1996; Sperry, 1993; Tobias, 1996).

Client-Centric Contexts

There have also been several studies, from the perspective of the client, as to why clients engage in professional coaching and more specifically the issues and or developmental goals the clients need help with the most (Hall, Otazo, & Hollenbeck, 1999). Even more impressive and now replete in the literature has been the rise in impact studies, again from the perspective of the client, that seek to understand the benefits and or outcomes of the professional coaching experience (Kampa-Kokesch & Anderson, 2010; McGovern et al., 2001; Wasylyshyn, 2003).

Despite this empirical focus on the client, little is known about those responsibilities, motivations, characteristics, and other competencies responsible for influencing the effectiveness of a professional coaching experience. As a result, the list of the client characteristics is noticeably shorter than the review of the coach-centric skills and characteristics. The client characteristics' list begins with the most current studies and works backwards chronologically. Several studies had only one competency to report, and on those occasions, they were coupled with other studies from different years, as a way to cluster the findings. Many researchers similarly reported the need for clients to identify and set clear developmental objectives (Hall et al., 1999).

Stevens (2005) identified the following client-centric characteristics in his study:

1. Being fully present for each coaching session.
2. Keeping appointments and commitments. Following through on completing their homework assignments.
3. Practicing new skills and behaviors needed for their development.
4. Taking an active role in involving all of their stakeholders (supporters and non-supporters) in the feedback process to ensure that they receive a full and real snapshot of how others perceive them.
5. Trusting their boss and organization's motives for enrolling them in coaching.
6. Choosing to see professional coaching as an opportunity to take advantage of.
7. Stopping to reflect and recognize their efforts and celebrating their successes along the way.
8. Being the best coach for that particular client.
9. Taking risks and doing whatever it takes to make changes.

Stevens (2005) reported adherence as a critical client-centric characteristic that leads to effective professional coaching. According to Stevens (2005), the term *adherence* comes from clinical psychology and refers to the "willingness of the client to engage and remain focused in the therapy. Applied to coaching, the client enters the coaching engagement with the idea that he or she will benefit and that he or she will engage the coach and the process" (p. 85). Stevens' emphasis on adherence is supported by the extensive work of Goldsmith, Lyons, and Freas (2000), while Ducharme (2004) states "it is a strong requirement of the coaching process that those who enter into a relationship with a professional coach are committed to the relationship and feel comfortable with the format and process" (p. 130). McGovern, Lindemann, Vergara, Murphy, Barker, and Warrenfeltz (2001) discuss the need for clients to voluntarily set and commit to their coaching goals.

Bush (2004) reported several client-centric findings in her research that were central to increasing the effectiveness of a professional coaching experience:

- Having realistic expectations of what they are actually able to accomplish—gain.
- Being conscious of not trying to change or improve in too many areas at once.
- Being "coachable" and open to the results of the feedback from the coach.
- Considering their coach's ideas, influence, and perspective of his or her behavioral and performance issues.
- Breaking down and working on the client's developmental goals in concrete, measurable steps.
- Holding the focus of the client's developmental goals and not allowing themselves to be sidetracked by other organizational distractions and "crises."
- Taking the time and making the effort to clarify upfront what the client needs/wants from the coaching experience and setting clear developmental goals.

Bush (2004) summarized her findings by stating, "[T]he client brings motivation, willingness to be coached, openness to the process, and a commitment to do the work" (p. xi).

Sztucinski (2001) identified several additional client-centric characteristics as influencing the effectiveness of his or her executive coaching experience:

1. Committed to coaching & doing the work (making time for the process, doing the homework, following up, and practicing new skills and behaviors).
2. Healthy and mature (client is psychologically mature and healthy enough to engage in the process).
3. Ready to learn/develop (client drive/motivation for learning; resolving issues and developing potential is present; open to feedback and capable of considering performance issues from a different point of view; open to coach's influence and help).

4. Capable of clarifying/setting coaching goals (client is capable of clarifying upfront what is needed/wanted from the coaching; is able to set clear developmental goals).

Coach Skills and Degrees of Professional Coaching Effectiveness Study

Based on what has been reported in the scholarly literature discussed in this chapter, a list of coaching characteristics and skills was created that respondents could compare against each other and identify which they believed to be most important in achieving professional coaching effectiveness (Boysen-Rotelli, 2012). This study included 157 ICF credentialed coaches and 70 of their clients who were surveyed and asked to use a Likert scale to identify the effectiveness (*very effective, effective,* or *somewhat effective, not effective*) of the outlined characteristics and skills. Table 6.1 outlines the results of this study, showcasing the top seven coaching and client characteristics and skills that were identified.

TABLE 6.1 Coach and Client Characteristics	
Coach Characteristics **(top seven by frequency & percentage)**	**Client Characteristics** **(top seven by frequency & percentage)**
Asks relevant, probing questions and gets the client to process their thoughts and ideas. ($n = 114$, 75.5%)	Being fully present for each coaching session. ($n = 117$, 77.5%)
Makes the client feel safe and can enable the client to trust the coach with issues of confidentiality. ($n = 114$, 75.5%)	Taking the time and making the effort to clarify upfront what they need/want from the coaching experience and setting clear developmental goals. ($n = 120$, 79.5%)
Challenges the client to think about new ideas and perspectives. ($n = 105$, 69.5%)	Taking risks and doing whatever it takes to makes changes. ($n = 11$, 73.5%)
Coaches the whole client and pays attention to the interaction between the client's professional and personal life. ($n = 96$, 63.6%)	Practicing new skills and behaviors needed for their development. ($n = 99$, 65.6%)
Holds the client accountable for doing the work. Insists that the client takes action and creates results. ($n = 78$, 63.6%)	Breaking down and working on their developmental goals in concrete, measurable steps. ($n = 93$, 61.6%)
Is non-judgmental, caring and supportive of the client's situation and needs. ($n = 78$, 51.7%)	Being "coachable" and open to the results of the feedback from the coach. Considering the coach's ideas, influence and perspective of their behavioral and performance issues. ($n = 93$, 61.6%)
Helps the client to identify and set clear developmental objectives, goals and assignments. ($n = 75$, 49.7%)	Stopping to reflect and recognize their efforts and celebrating their successes along the way. ($n = 63$, 41.7%)

The Coaching Characteristics Effectiveness Model

Figure 6.1 presents the coaching effectiveness model developed as a result of the Coach Skills and Degrees of Professional Coaching Effectiveness Study (Boysen-Rotelli, 2012). The figure cites each of the top seven skills and competencies for both the coach and the client.

Alignment With the Core Competencies

There is direct alignment between these coaching skills and the ICF core competencies. This can be seen in Table 6.2. The alignment between the ICF core competencies and the skills that are part of the coaching effectiveness model is clear. These additional skills are not in conflict with the 11 core competencies, but rather, they complement them and support them deeply.

The Coach Skills and Degrees of Professional Coaching Effectiveness Study sought to better understand the systemic nature within the complexity of the executive coaching experience by exploring and describing the multiple skills and characteristics that are necessary for effectiveness in an executive coaching experience, from the coach's and client's perspective (Boysen-Rotelli, 2012). This study has taken the field one-step further with scholarly research about the skills and characteristics that lead to effectiveness. In total, this study utilized the voice of 157 ICF coaches to represent, through the coaching effectiveness model, the most important skills and characteristics for executive coaching effectiveness.

The findings of this nonexperimental descriptive study presents the top seven most commonly cited coach and client competencies, from the coach's perspective, necessary for executive coaching effectiveness. The coaching effectiveness model provides the coach, the client, the organization sponsoring the client's development, or the researcher a quantitative bird's-eye view of what has been identified as necessary for effectiveness in the coaching engagement. As mentioned in Chapter 1, this study and the findings of this study have addressed the requests of researchers calling for more systemic approaches to exploring the complexity of executive coaching. To this end, the results of this present study have brought into focus a view of the entire executive coaching effectiveness phenomenon.

Chapter Summary

There is no question that the executive coach is the lynchpin of the executive coaching experience, working hard to ensure improved client

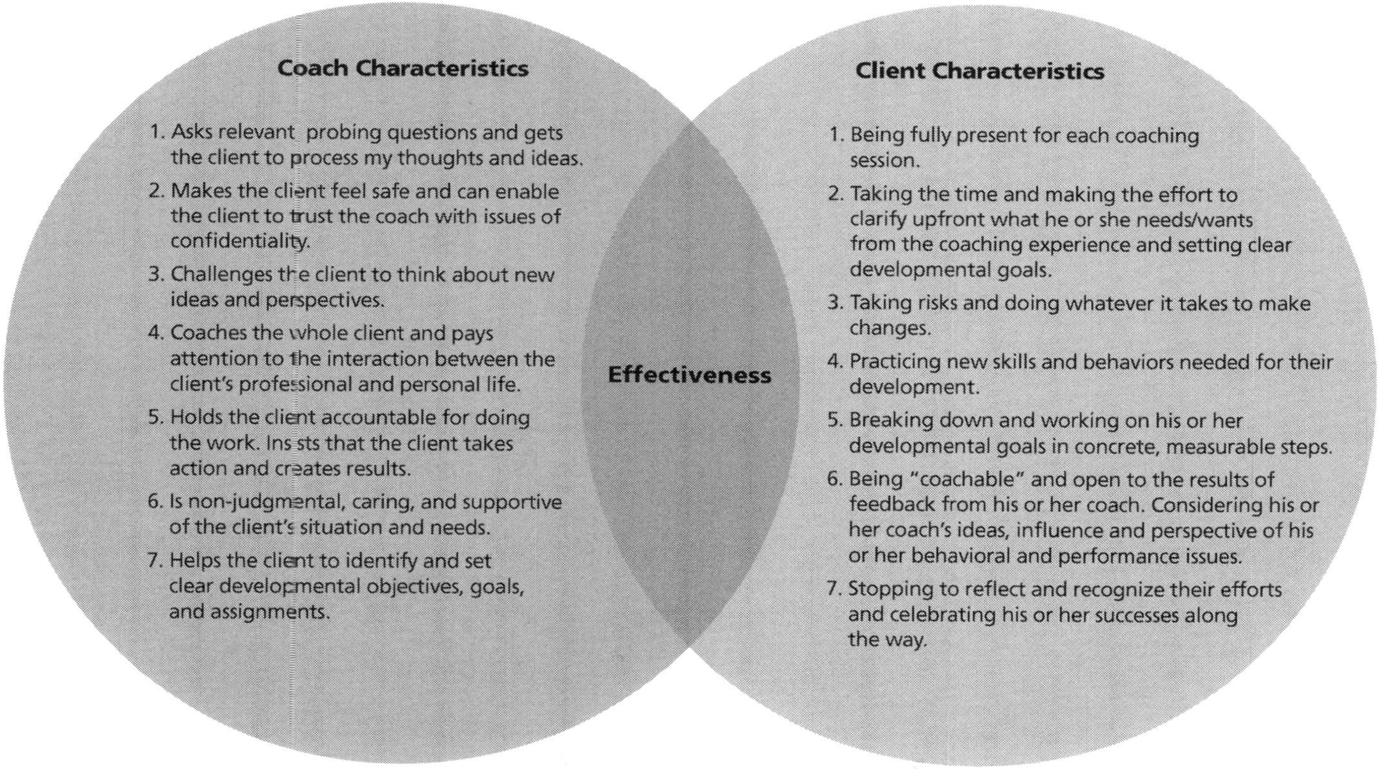

Coach Characteristics

1. Asks relevant probing questions and gets the client to process my thoughts and ideas.
2. Makes the client feel safe and can enable the client to trust the coach with issues of confidentiality.
3. Challenges the client to think about new ideas and perspectives.
4. Coaches the whole client and pays attention to the interaction between the client's professional and personal life.
5. Holds the client accountable for doing the work. Insists that the client takes action and creates results.
6. Is non-judgmental, caring, and supportive of the client's situation and needs.
7. Helps the client to identify and set clear developmental objectives, goals, and assignments.

Client Characteristics

1. Being fully present for each coaching session.
2. Taking the time and making the effort to clarify upfront what he or she needs/wants from the coaching experience and setting clear developmental goals.
3. Taking risks and doing whatever it takes to make changes.
4. Practicing new skills and behaviors needed for their development.
5. Breaking down and working on his or her developmental goals in concrete, measurable steps.
6. Being "coachable" and open to the results of feedback from his or her coach. Considering his or her coach's ideas, influence and perspective of his or her behavioral and performance issues.
7. Stopping to reflect and recognize their efforts and celebrating his or her successes along the way.

Effectiveness

Figure 6.1 Coaching Effectiveness Model. *Source:* Boysen-Rotelli, 2012.

TABLE 6.2   ICF Core Competencies Alignment With the Skills in the Coaching Effectiveness Model

ICF Core Competencies	Coaching Effectiveness Model
Powerful Questioning	Asks relevant, probing questions and gets the client to process his or her thoughts and ideas.
Establishing Trust and Intimacy with the Client Meeting Ethical Guidelines and Professional Standards	Makes the client feel safe and can enable the client to trust the coach with issues of confidentiality.
Direct Communication	Challenges the client to think about new ideas and perspectives.
Establishing the Coaching Agreement	Coaches the whole client and pays attention to the interaction between the client's professional and personal life.
Managing Progress and Accountability Designing Actions	Holds the client accountable for doing the work. Insists that the client take action and create results.
Active Listening Coaching Presence	Is non-judgmental, caring and supportive of the client's situation and needs.
Planning and Goal Setting Creating Awareness	Helps the client to identify and set clear developmental objectives, goals and assignments.

performance and that the client doesn't slip off of his or her developmental pathway. There's a stark reality however, that the executive coach is the *developmental leader* and he or she can only lead the client to the proverbial *developmental water*. The results of this study should serve as a reminder that executive coaching effectiveness is contingent upon not only a good coach, but that the client must also engage fully in the work and sometimes this work is hard. Given the overabundance of practice and academic literature swirling around the executive coach, there seems to be a developmental laziness or belief that the client's answers reside "out there or with the coach." Maybe clients, as recipients and beneficiaries of the service, will begin to hold themselves more accountable as the messages in the marketplace begin to communicate that they themselves can make or break the executive coaching effectiveness equation.

Chapter Reflection Questions

1. What other coaching research would help to further establish the coaching profession?
2. What do you feel are the most important coaching skills and characteristics? Why?

3. What does coaching effectiveness mean to you? What does it mean to your clients?

Activity

Ask your clients what they feel the most important characteristics and skills are when being coached. Consider developing your own effectiveness model that you can use to explain coaching to your clients.

References

Boysen-Rotelli, S. (2012). *Executive Coaching Effectiveness: A Qualitative Study* (Doctoral dissertation). Retrieved from ProQuest (3537382).

Brotman, L. E., Liberi, W. P., & Wasylyshyn, K. M. (1998). Professional coaching: The need for standards of competence. *Consulting Psychology Journal: Practice and Research, 40*(1), 40–46.

Bush, M. (2004). *Client perceptions of effectiveness in executive coaching* (Doctoral dissertation, Pepperdine University, 2004). Dissertation Abstracts International, A66, 04. (UMI No.3171835)

Corporate Leadership Council. (2017). [Summary of research: Professional coaching]. Unpublished raw data.

Diedrich, R. C., & Kilburg, R. R. (2001). Foreword: Further consideration of executive coaching as an emerging competency. *Consulting Psychology Journal: Practice and Research, 53*(4), 203–204.

Ducharme, M. J. (2004). The cognitive-behavioral approach to professional coaching. *Consulting Psychology Journal: Practice and Research, 56*(4), 214–224.

Grant, A. M. (2007). A languishing-flourishing model of goal striving and mental health for coaching populations. *International Coaching Psychology Review, 2*(3), 250–264.

Goldsmith, M., Lyons, L., & Freas, A. (Eds.). (2000). *Coaching for leadership: How the world's greatest coaches help leaders learn.* San Francisco, CA: John Wiley and Sons.

Hall, D. T., Otazo, K. L., & Hollenbeck, G. P. (1999). Behind closed doors: What really happens in professional coaching. *Organizational Dynamics, 27*(3), 39–54.

International Coach Federation. (2017). *Coaching core competencies.* Retrieved May 17, 2017 from https://coachfederation.org/faqs

Judge, W. Q., & Cowell, J. (1997, July/August). The brave new world of professional coaching. *Business Horizons,* 71–77.

Kampa-Kokesch, S., & Anderson, M. Z. (2010). Professional coaching: A comprehensive review of literature. *Consulting Psychology Journal: Practice and Research, 53*(4), 205–228.

Kilburg, R. R. (1996). Toward a conceptual understanding and definition of professional coaching. *Consulting Psychology Journal: Practice and Research, 48*(2), 134–144.

Levinson, H. (1996). Executive coaching. *Consulting Psychology Journal: Practice and Research, 48*(2), 115–123.

McGovern, J., Lindemann, M., Vergara, M., Murphy, S., Barker, L., & Warrenfeltz, R. (2001). Maximizing the impact of professional coaching: Behavioral change, organizational outcomes, and return on investment. *The Manchester Review, 6*(1), 1–9.

Saporito, T. J. (1996). Business-linked professional development: Coaching senior professionals. *Consulting Psychology Journal: Practice and Research, 48*(2), 96–103.

Sperry, L. (1993). Working with professionals: Consulting, counseling, and coaching. *Individual Psychology, 49*(2), 257–267.

Stevens, J. H., Jr. (2005). Professional coaching from the professional's perspective. *Consulting Psychology Journal: Practice and Research, 57*(4), 274–285.

Sztucinski, K. (2001). *The nature of executive coaching: An exploration of the executive's experience.* The George Washington University, Wahington, DC.

Tobias, L. L. (1996). Coaching professionals. *Consulting Psychology Journal: Practice and Research, 48*(2), 87–95.

Wasylyshyn, K. M. (2003). Professional coaching: An outcome study. *Consulting Psychology Journal: Practice and Research, 55*(2), 94–106.

7

The Use of Assessments in Coaching

This chapter provides an overview of how to use assessments in a coaching relationship. Assessments are often used in coaching to develop the client's awareness, to jump-start the initial phase of coaching, and to provide data for goal setting and return on investment. Numerous assessments are available to coaches, some at no cost and others costing hundreds of dollars or more. The decision of a coach to incorporate assessments into their practice may depend on the types of coaching clients that the coach works with, the kinds of assessments that the coach has found personally valuable, and the coach's overall familiarity with assessments. One of the most effective ways for coaches to explore assessments and their value is through leveraging some of these assessment tools for themselves to evaluate the relevance and the value they provide for them and their client.

The focus of this chapter will be on varied tools including those that enhance personal awareness, and tools to enhance work-related, leadership, team, and organizational awareness. It is important to understand the range of assessments available, choose assessments that enable clients to enhance their awareness and set goals, identify assessments that are a best

An Introduction to Professional and Executive Coaching, pages 95–106
Copyright © 2018 by Information Age Publishing

fit based on a particular coaching issue, and use powerful questions that enable clients to most effectively use assessment results.

Using Feedback in Coaching

Although the essence of coaching is asking powerful questions that generate new and important levels of awareness, there are times when feedback is acceptable and helpful for clients. One of the most relevant areas for feedback in coaching comes from the use of assessments. An assessment and its results can be very valuable, but often, the true value comes from receiving feedback about the assessment results from a coach who is familiar with and/or has training in administering and debriefing the assessment.

Table 7.1 summarizes the research on the practice of feedback. Passmore (2008) organized his research into four important categories on the link between feedback and performance, the feedback sender, the feedback message, and the feedback recipient. There is not a single widely accepted model for giving feedback. However, the process of feedback includes a few elements: the sender of the message, the recipient of the message, and the message itself.

Figure 7.1 depicts a general model of giving and receiving feedback. The sender is the one who initiates the feedback. There is a message that

TABLE 7.1 Summary of the Research on Feedback From Passmore (2008)	
Research Topic	**Key Findings**
Link between feedback and performance	Non-consistent; performance can increase as well as decrease following feedback (Kluger & DeNisi, 1996)
The feedback sender	This could be a number of sources: a single individual, several individuals, a task, or the self. Not all feedback sources have the same impact: it is important that the source is credible. (Bastos & Fletcher, 1995)
The feedback message	People like receiving and giving praise (Anseel and Lievens, 2006), but are less comfortable with criticism; however, it cannot be concluded that praise will always have a positive impact, and criticism will always have a negative impact. The message has more impact if it is linked to goals.
The feedback recipient	People interpret feedback subjectively, in their own frame of reference (Ilgen, Fisher & Taylor, 1979); any behavior change following feedback depends on individuals' characteristics such as their self-esteem (Shrauger and Rosenberg, 1970) and their belief in their capabilities (Renn & Fedor, 2001). People need feedback to be motivated to learn from feedback, otherwise behaviors are unlikely to change

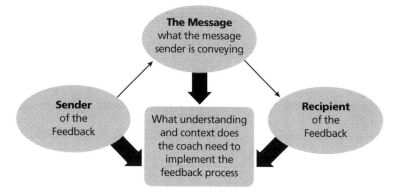

Figure 7.1 General feedback model. *Source:* Adapted from Passmore (2008).

needs to be communicated, and then the message is understood and discussed by the sender and the recipient. In the context of coaching engagements, the feedback could be coming from the coach who is presenting the information and interpreting the assessment results to the client. Or it could be coming from other managers and colleagues in the context of a multi-rater or 360-degree feedback assessment that collects feedback from individuals that the client being assessed works with. The senders of a message have control over different aspects of the feedback such as their own personal style of delivering communication. In professional coaching engagements, the feedback sender, at least in part, is the coach. The recipient of the feedback, in a coaching engagement, is the client. The biggest challenge with giving feedback is that individuals all receive feedback differently. Some people will take feedback very well while others will not. This is important because the feedback message may need to be tailored depending on the individual receiving the feedback.

The feedback message is the information that the sender is relaying to the recipient. In the context of coaching, this message will depend greatly on the type of assessment that is being debriefed. In multi-rater or 360-degree feedback assessment work, the message is related to the work, the effectiveness of the individual being assessed, and the working relationship of the client.

Feedback is a large part of the assessment debriefing process; however, feedback also takes place less formally throughout the entire coaching engagement. As this happens, the coach and the client continue to design, assess goals and progress during the coaching process.

To be effective, feedback needs to be clear and concise, as well as be linked to the goals of the client. A number of studies have looked at the

TABLE 7.2 Specific vs. General Goals and Feedback in Coaching

Feedback in coaching	Goals set within the Coaching Engagement	
	Specific	**General**
Specific	Feedback is easily understood by the client and results in future learning.	Subsequent evaluation of any goal is difficult.
General	Feedback is interpreted within the recipient's frame of reference (how he or she sees the world) and is unlikely to result in behavioral change.	Feedback is difficult to interpret and apply for the client.

effectiveness of feedback. The findings align with the idea that the more goal focused and specific the feedback is, the more effective it will be (Locke & Latham, 2012). Table 7.2 shows how goals and level of generalization can link with feedback in a coaching engagement.

Criteria for Assessment Tools

There are several criteria that are important to consider when using an assessment with coaching. These include:

- quantitative measurement of the assessment,
- ease of use of the assessment, and
- development: theory/conceptual base of the assessment.

Quantitative Measurement of the Assessment

Three of the most important quantitative considerations of an assessment include reliability, validity, and norms. Reliability is the consistency of test scores from one point of measurement to the next. Test-retest reliability and internal consistency are sub-measures of reliability. Validity is the evidence that supports that a tool measures what it says it does—construct validity (convergent, discriminant) and criterion validity (predictive and concurrent). Norms are existing data on test takers that allow for the comparison of one individual's score to those of a large group to aid in interpretation. Table 7.3 defines these important quantitative measures.

Errors of measurement include various kinds of errors associated with a test score that may impact the interpretation of scores. How can the influence of any extraneous factors that are unrelated to what the assessment is attempting to measure be reduced or eliminated (e.g., test-taking concerns, desire to appear in a favorable light, familiarity with the measure)?

TABLE 7.3   Assessment Reliability and Validity

Psychometric property	Definition
Reliability	The stability and consistency of test results.
Test–retest reliability	The stability of test results over repeated administration of the test.
Internal consistency	The extent to which test items that measure the same attribute are related to each other.
Construct validity	The extent to which a measure accurately assesses the attribute it intends to assess.
Convergent validity	The extent to which test scores are related to scores on alternative tests or measures of the same attributes.
Discrimination validity	The extent to which test scores are unrelated to scores on alternative tests or measures of different attributes.
Criterion-related validity	The relationship between test scores and measure of an independent outcome.
Predictive validity	The correlation between a test score and an outcome measure that is gathered at a later point in time.
Concurrent validity	The correlation between a test score and an outcome measure that is collected at the same point in time.
Norm group and normative data	The sample of the population that participated in the development and validation of the test. This group's test results provide the average distribution of scores against which future test takers can be compared.

However, in the context of coaching, an assessment is not necessarily a poor tool if it's not rigorously developed. It often depends on the goals of coaching as they align with the assessment as well as the ease of use of the tool.

Ease of Use of the Assessment

Ease of use refers to how easy the assessment is to access, complete, and debrief. This may relate to how much training and credentialing is required to use the assessment tool or how expensive the tool is to administer. Many assessment tools require extensive financial investment both from the perspective of training to become certified or credentialed to administer, or in the cost to purchase the assessment for individual administration.

Theory/Conceptual Base of the Assessment

The third consideration is the theoretical framework that supports the assessment. Assessments such as the VIA (Values in Action) Signature Strengths Profile, for example, have extensive theoretical backing by extensive research conducted at the University of Pennsylvania.

Proper Use of Assessments

Leveraging the best assessment in a coaching relationship depends on the goals of the coaching. It is also important to make sure that the assessment is being used in an appropriate and ethical manner. The International Test Commission (ITC) Guidelines on Test Use (2013) provides a framework of standards that should be considered when using assessment tests. This checklist is summarized in Table 7.4.

Any assessment used in the coaching engagement should be selected carefully and should clearly align with the client's goals for the coaching engagement. Proper use of an assessment involves determining if the characteristics of the tool are appropriate for the intended use and client, and are of adequate technical quality (rigor) for this use. Other criteria for selecting may include cost, timing, and quality/history of use as well as norms if needed, and whether or not a credential is needed to administer and interpret it.

When the assessment requires specific accreditation or certification, it is imperative that the coach has met those requirements or is leveraging a secondary party that is a qualified user of the assessment to administer and debrief the assessment. A qualified user is someone who possesses the appropriate training, education, and experience in using the assessment for the purpose for which it is being used. According to the Standards for Educational and Psychological Testing, qualifications of test users depend on

TABLE 7.4 Summary of Checklist for Ethical Testing
1. Define the purpose of the assessment.
2. Determine the kinds of tests that will best address the purpose of the assessment.
3. Select the best test for your purpose.
4. Select only those tests that you are competent in and trained to administer and interpret.
5. Gather relevant collateral information to better understand the context in which the assessment is being conducted.
6. Consider who will receive feedback and report the assessment and gain informed consent from the client.
7. Ensure that the client understands the purpose of the assessment and how the results will be used.
8. Make adequate arrangements to ensure standardized administration.
9. Take account of any factors that may impact the client's ability to complete the assessment.
10. Be aware of your ethical and professional responsibility, and the rights and responsibilities of coaches who undertake the assessment.

the specific situation and user. This means that each assessment user must evaluate his or her qualifications and competence for selecting, administering, scoring, interpreting, reporting, or communicating assessment results. An assessment user must develop the skills and knowledge for each test that he or she intends to use.

An additional consideration is the use of the assessment information: Who will own the data from this assessment tool? For example, will only the client have access to the information, or will an employer or other interested party also have access? It is important to address who will have access to the data at the onset of the coaching engagement prior to administering the assessment.

Types of Assessments

Before a coach begins to work with a client it is important to first introduce an assessment. This could potentially be part of the first session to help formulate goals or direction for the coaching. It could be used as a benchmark prior to the start of coaching to use as a measure to assess the success of the coaching during or after the coaching engagement. It can be a great tool to use at the onset of coaching to build trust and rapport by building some understanding of the client and who he or she is as a person or what his or her goals are. Assessment can also be used to evaluate change. Using the same tool at multiple points in time provides the client with "evidence" of his or her progress. This could also be a potential measure of return on investment (ROI). An assessment can also be used as the basis for deciding whether to continue coaching based on the results and progress that the assessment shows. Lastly, an assessment can be used to help a client get unstuck. An assessment can shine a light on areas that a client may not be aware of or shift the way in which you are coaching and get you out of your coaching ruts.

Personality and Style Assessments

There is an abundance of personality assessments and questionnaires that exist measuring both broad and narrow sets of individual preferences and behavior. Measuring dimensions of the personality and personal preference are beneficial in a coaching engagement to help build the client's awareness of his or her way or mode of thinking as well as his or her behavior across numerous different settings and situations. This type of assessment can contribute to explaining why some individuals are well suited to some types of work or environments while others are not as well suited. It can also explain why some environments or situations can cause more stress for some individuals than for others.

Frequently Used Personal Style Tools

DISC. Focuses on how people do things. The four dimensions that are addressed are: dominance, influencing, steadiness, and compliance.

Clifton Strengths Finder. The Clifton Strengths Finder measures the presence of talents in 34 general areas referred to as themes. Talents are ways in which we naturally think, feel, and behave as unique individuals, and they serve as the foundation of strengths development.

MBTI. The MBTI is an assessment of personal preferences for being in the world (introversion or extroversion), seeing things (sensing or intuitive), decision making (feeling or thinking), and degree of closure desired (judging or perceiving).

Vocation and Motivational Needs/Values Assessments

Vocational or career assessments can be very helpful in shedding light on professional fields of employment and occupations that are of good fit for individuals. Career and vocational assessments often ask questions about what people enjoy doing in multiple dimensions of their life outside of work which helps to create greater awareness and potential for exploring work in the context of what clients enjoy in all areas of their life. Occupational preferences are closely linked to personality style (Holland, 1997). For this reason, it is helpful to combine vocation or career assessments with other assessments during the coaching assessment process.

The assessment of motivational needs and values is one of the lesser defined areas of assessment. This may be due to the multitude of motivational theories and models that exist. However, there is still value in this area of assessment. It can particularly be of value to clients who need clarity about the types of environments or cultures that would be a good fit for them, or if they are dissatisfied with their current work environment and would like to gain clarity about what would be a good fit for them.

Frequently Used Vocation and Values Tools

Strong Interest Inventory. The goal of this assessment is to give insight into a person's interests, so that he or she may have less difficulty in deciding on an appropriate career choice for himself or herself.

VIA. Identifies your top 5 strengths out of 34 possibilities; enables you to generate an action plan online.

Multi-Rater/360 Tools for Assessment

Some of the most comprehensive types of assessments are assessments that have multiple points of input and rating. These are usually known as multi-rater or 360-degree feedback assessments. They are defined by the multiple points of feedback and assessment that come from individuals at various levels of the organization in relation to the individual that the assessment is being conducted for. This feedback can come from leaders, managers, peers, members of other departments, direct reports, suppliers (or others that work closely with the individual from outside the organization), or even customers.

This type of assessment provides a comprehensive and valid measure of workplace behavior. It creates an opportunity for learning through feedback from different perspectives and vantage points which allows individuals to see valuable opportunities to change and engage in relevant follow-up and development opportunities. Also, feedback from these multiple sources can provide valuable information that the individual may not have without this opportunity for feedback and assessment.

Frequently Used Multi-Rater/360-degree Feedback Tools:

- Leadership Circle 360,
- TILT 360,
- Conflict Dynamics Profile (CDP),
- Leadership Culture Survey,
- Leadership Practices Inventory (LPI), and
- EQ-360.

Additional Assessment Tools

Examples of Personal Style/Personality Tools:

- Enneagram
- FIRO-B
- Locus of control
- Strong Interest Inventory
- Myers Briggs Type Indicator (MBTI)
- Multiple intelligences (e.g., Joyce Bishop, PhD's Pathways to Learning)
- Gregorc Styles
- PIAV
- Strengths Finder 2.0 (Rath, 2007)

- DISC
- Hogan
- Winslow

Examples of Work Approach Tools:

- Change Style Indicator
- Communication Styles inventory
- TKI
- Leadership Style
- Work/Management balance wheel (in Coactive Coaching)

Examples of 360-Degree Tools:

- BarOn Emotional Intelligence EQ360
- Leadership Practices Inventory
- Benchmarks (Center for Creative Leadership)
- Conflict Dynamics Profile (Eckerd College)
- The Leadership Circle (The Leadership Circle)
- The Birkman Method (Birkman)

Examples of Organizational assessment tools:

- The Leadership Culture Survey
- Team Diagnostic
- "Trust Survey for Schools" (Tschannen-Moran, 2004)

Examples of Free (or Nearly Free) Assessments

- Balance wheel, and many others (Whitworth, Kimsey-House, & Sandahl, 2010; accompanying CD).
- Clean Sweep (available at www.Coachville.com, http://www.betterme.org/cleansweep.html, and various online sites)
- Explore your Values (Pavlina, 2004a, 2004b)

Examples of Books With Assessments

- "Scrubdown" (and various other tools; Blanchard & Homan, 2004).
- "Test Your Own Optimism" (Seligman, 1998).
- "What's Your Procrastination Type: The Six Styles of Procrastination and How to Overcome Them" (Sapadin & Maguire, 1996).

Chapter Summary

Well-developed assessments can be useful tools for coaches to use to support their clients' development and contribute to the development of greater client awareness gained from the understanding, reflection, and self-exploration that comes from assessment data. Coaches need to have a deep understanding of the theoretical and intended use of each assessment used. Although some assessments require extensive training to administer, there are some valuable assessment tools that can be used without specific training or credentialing. The inappropriate and unskilled use of assessment tools can contribute to the reduced credibility of the individual coach and the coaching profession. Therefore, it is of utmost importance that coaches use assessment responsibly and ethically.

Chapter Reflection Questions

1. What are the potential barriers or concerns in using assessments?
2. What criteria should be used to decide on the most appropriate assessment to use in a given situation, for a specific client?
3. What role does feedback play in a coaching conversation?

Activity

Complete some of the assessments listed throughout this chapter. Reflect on the value of these assessments and how you can use them with coaching clients.

References

Anseel, F., & Lievens, F. (2006). Certainty as a moderator of feedback reactions? A test of the strength of the self-verification motive. *Journal of Occupational Psychology, 79,* 533–551.

Bastos, M., & Fletcher, C. (1995). Exploring the individual's perception of sources and credibility of feedback in the work environment. *International Journal of Selection and Assessment, 3*(1), 29–39.

Blanchard, S., & Homan, M. (2004). *Leverage Your Best, Ditch the Rest.* New York, NY: William Morrow.

Holland, J. L. (1997). *Educational Opportunities Finder.* Odessa, FL: Psychological Assessment Resources.

Ilgen, D., Fisher, D., & Taylor, M. (1979). Consequences of individual feedback on behavior in organizations, *Journal of Applied Psychology, 64,* 349–371.

International Test Commission. (2013). *ITC guidelines on test usage.* Retrieved from https://www.intestcom.org/files/guideline_test_use.pdf

Kluger, A., & DeNisi, A. (1996). The effects of feedback interventions on performance: A historical review, a meta-analysis and a preliminary feedback intervention theory. *Psychological Bulletin, 119,* 254–284.

Locke, E., & Latham, G. (2012). *A Theory of Goal Setting and Task Performance.* Englewood Cliffs, NJ: Prentice Hall.

Passmore, J. (2008). *Psychometrics in Coaching.* Philadelphia, PA: Kogan-Page.

Pavlina, S. (2004a). *List of values.* Retrieved from http://www.stevepavlina.com/articles/list-of-values.htm

Pavlina, S. (2004b). *Living your values, Part I.* Retrieved from http://www.steve pavlina.com/articles/living-your-values-1.htm

Rath, T. (2007) *StrengthsFinder 2.0 : A new and updated edition of the online test from Gallup's Now, Discover Your Strengths.* Washington, DC: Gallup Press.

Renn, R., & Fedor, D. (2001). Development and field test of a feedback seeking, self-efficacy, and goal setting model of work performance, *Journal of Management, 27*(5), 563–583.

Sapadin, L., & Maguire, J. (1996). *It's About Time.* New York, NY: Penguin Books.

Seligman, M. (1998). *Learned Optimism: How to Change Your Mind and Your Life.* New York, NY: Free Press.

Shrauger, J., & Rosenberg, S. (1970). Self-esteem and the effects of success and failure feedback on performance. *Journal of Personality and Social Psychology, 38,* 404–417.

Tschannen-Moran, M. (2004). *Trust matters: Leadership for successful schools.* San Francisco, CA: Jossey-Bass.

Whitworth, L., Kimsey-House, K., Kimsey-House, H., & Sandahl, P. (2010). *Co-active coaching.* Mountain View, CA: Davies Black.

8

Establishing Your Practice

This chapter addresses specific and actionable information about how to start, grow, and maintain a strong and successful coaching business. It will start with the basics, including the importance of developing a coaching specialty and identifying your target market. It will also cover specific pricing and marketing strategies for a coaching business. The tools and strategies provided in this chapter will help coaches build and sustain a successful coaching practice.

Developing Your Specialty

Having a target market is one of the best things that a coach can do to start and grow his or her business. A true formula to fail is to attempt to be "everything to everyone." It is important to specialize and hone in on a specific target market—the market that you feel is your ideal client. In fact, the more specifically a coach defines his or her niche or coaching specialty, the easier it will be to find clients. Many coaches feel that limiting their potential market, especially when they are just starting out, will limit

An Introduction to Professional and Executive Coaching, pages 107–113
Copyright © 2018 by Information Age Publishing

their business. However, that is not the case! A coach needs to be specific so they can market more effectively and reach that specific audience more effectively. When coaches specialize, it becomes more evident to potential clients that the coach will be specifically able to help them.

No matter how specific you define a coaching specialty, it is always possible to expand that specialty to other areas in the future. You will never be "locked in" to a specialty and can always reassess and decide if you would like to change or expand your specialty. When developing a specialty for coaching, it is important to think about who and what your coaching will support. Your target market is your "who." A target market is about defining the demographics or breaking down a market into a specific segment of characteristics. This breakdown might be by occupation, age, a profession, or it could be a combination of any or all of the above as well as other characteristics.

A target market is defined by a combination of the following characteristics:

- *Demographics:* gender, age, income, education, race, family status, religion, profession, social affiliations, and so on.
- *Field/Industry:* technology, healthcare, retail, hospitality, education, and so on.
- *Job/Position:* executives, salespeople, mid-level managers, accountants, attorneys, artists, business owners, and so on.
- *An Identifiable Situation:* career changers, empty nesters, entrepreneurs, cancer or people in recovery from a recent setback of some type, and so on.
- *Geographic Information:* where they live, where you can reach them, and so on.
- Personal Characteristics: traits, abilities, skills, interests, passions, and so on.

Target Market Examples

Table 8.1 lists examples of target markets. You can see examples of how you can move from general to very specific with your target market. A great place to start is by thinking about the results that people want and concerns that people already have. The "what" of the coaching are the results the coaching provides, the benefits the coaching provides, or the problem the coaching solves. This is the opposite of trying to be all things to all people. Your "what" is your coaching specialty.

Some examples of a coaching specialty might include:

- time management,

TABLE 8.1 Examples of Target Markets

General	More Specific	Very Specific
Women in transition	Stay-at-home moms in transition	Stay-at-home moms in transition in their 30s
Small business owners	Small business owners of service businesses	Small business owners of service businesses who have been in business for more than 5 years
People making a career change	Recent MBA graduates that are looking to make a career change	Recent MBA graduates that are looking to make a career change and hold a liberal arts undergraduate degree

- stress reduction,
- finance,
- career change,
- business or professional, and
- executive or leadership.

Pricing and Packaging

There are two main ways that coaches typically charge for their services. They can charge an hourly or per-session rate or they can charge a monthly fee for services. Many coaches feel a three-step pricing model works the best. Specifically, this is based on a monthly fee and features three different coaching packages that a client can choose from: a low-priced option, a medium-priced option, and a higher-priced premium option.

The highest priced offering typically provides the most coaching and the highest level of service. It is designed for clients who like to buy the best and want to receive the maximum level of service that you offer. For example, this package may contain 4 calls per month and unlimited check-ins via email and by phone.

The medium-priced package is what you want and expect the majority of clients to choose. For example, this package may contain 3 calls per month and unlimited check-ins via email.

The low-priced option is designed to accommodate clients that you really want to coach, but who are not able to invest in your other two packages. Having a low-priced option is extremely valuable for new coaches who are focused on gaining experience and building their client base. For example, this package may contain two calls per month and limited check-ins via email.

Marketing Your Coaching

There are three parts to a strong marketing process. Each part represents a different type of activity:

1. Active Marketing Strategies
2. Passive Marketing Strategies
3. "Follow Up" Marketing Strategies

All three parts of the marketing system are important for building and maintaining a strong coaching business. The key is knowing when to focus on each part of your marketing. Maximum effectiveness comes when you make smart and strategic decisions about how much time, energy, and money to invest in each part of your marketing process.

Active Marketing Strategies

These are the things you do (actively) to directly connect with potential clients. Active marketing requires action on the part of the business. Active marketing may mean networking with other businesses or working on building your referral pool. It also includes selective advertising to drive in new business. This type of marketing is deliberate and purposeful. It takes effort. Active marketing often includes meeting vendors and customers face to face, holding sales appointments, and making cold calls. This kind of marketing requires skill and persistence. Also, active marketing allows your potential clients to experience you in some way. In turn, this can help them to better see the value that you can provide.

Examples of Active Marketing Activities:

- Speaking (workshops, webinars, speaking engagements)
- Leveraging Your Existing Network
- Targeted Networking
- Writing Articles

Active marketing strategies are powerful because they give you exposure. Choose one or two active marketing strategies at any one time to focus on. Focus on doing one or two of them very well rather than trying to do too many things at a time.

Passive Marketing Strategies

You need and want passive marketing strategies; however, these are not things that bring your business in and of themselves. Passive marketing strategies complement active marketing strategies. Passive marketing reaches the customer through customer service and smart positioning. For example, a customer uses a search engine to locate a business. The marketing was done before the need arose, and no special event was required to bring the customer into the business. Passive marketing is thoughtful and anticipatory.

Examples of passive marketing strategies:

- Logo, Letterhead and Business Cards
- Website
- Published Articles
- Physical Products (book, audio CD, DVD)

Passive marketing strategies are important, but you need the active marketing strategies to jumpstart your business. If you are focused on getting more clients, don't spend too much time and energy on your passive marketing strategies, especially if it keeps you from engaging in active marketing. This is a mistake too many coaches make.

"Follow-Up" Marketing

Follow-up marketing is about relationship or database marketing, in other words, growing "your list." It is important to use follow-up marketing so you don't lose touch with any of your audience or potential clients.

Examples of follow up marketing strategies:

- Sending out an email or newsletter on a regular basis
- Using social media, such as Facebook, Twitter and LinkedIn
- Making regular follow-up phone calls to check in and add value

Keep in touch marketing is important because many of the people you connect with through your active marketing strategies will not be ready to hire you or invest in coaching when they first meet you.

Generating Referrals

A referral is someone who inquires about your coaching based on the recommendation of another person. The person that refers them may be someone who has already worked with you or is very familiar with your business. A referral-based business will still require some marketing; however, it requires far less time and energy than a business that does not have a strong referral network.

Below are two of the biggest benefits of creating a referral-based business. Reminding yourself why you want a referral-based business will help you take the necessary action and have the discipline to achieve it.

Stronger Leads That Are Ready to Begin Working With You

When a referral contacts you about your coaching there is a high likelihood that person is already "sold" at least on some level. The person who is referring your coaching usually set the foundation for you by informing the potential client about the benefits and the value of your coaching. This is so much more desirable than the process of converting a completely "cold" client to a paying client.

Maximizing Your Time and Minimizing Your Effort

When you build a healthy referral process you will be able to spend a little bit less time generating new business. You still need to check in with your network and nurture those relationships, but there isn't as much work and effort involved. This will free up additional time so you can focus more on your clients, increasing your skills and training, and simply enjoying your coaching.

When you focus on building a referral-based business, your main marketing activities include Two main priorities:

1. Providing great coaching, service, and value to your clients.
2. Educating, informing, and providing value to your network.

How to Generate More Referrals

Referrals can come from a variety of sources, including

- your current client base,
- your past/former clients, and
- your network (friends, family, neighbors, coworkers, classmates etc.).

Chapter Summary

Many coaches spend a significant amount of time, energy and resources learning the coaching skill set. However, they often struggle with putting this skill set to work for them from a business model standpoint. The strategies mentioned in this chapter will help new and existing coaches to build and/or strengthen their coaching practice. It is important to focus on a number of different strategies that attract, keep, and build a pipeline for future clients.

Chapter Reflection Questions

1. What are some of the best ways to determine your coaching niche and specialty?
2. What type of marketing strategies are you most comfortable with?
3. What type of referral strategies do you feel will work best for you?

Activity

Create a marketing plan for your coaching. Include a defined specialty/niche for your coaching. Map what your pricing and package structure will look like. What will be your active, passive, and keep in touch marketing strategies?

Appendix

International Coach Federation (ICF) Professional Certified Coach (PCC) Markers

Assessment markers are the indicators that an assessor is trained to listen for to determine which ICF core competencies are in evidence in a recorded coaching conversation, and to what extent. The following markers are the behaviors that should be exhibited in a coaching conversation at the professional certified coach (PCC) level. These markers support a performance evaluation process that is fair, consistent, valid, reliable, repeatable, and defensible. Please note these markers are not a tool for coaching, and should not be used as a checklist or formula for passing the performance evaluation.

Competency 1: Meeting Ethical Guidelines and Professional Standards

Understanding of coaching ethics and standards and ability to apply them appropriately in all coaching situations.

Competency 2: Creating the Coaching Agreement

1. Coach helps to identify, or reconfirm, what the client wants to accomplish in the session.

An Introduction to Professional and Executive Coaching, pages 115–118
Copyright © 2018 by Information Age Publishing
All rights of reproduction in any form reserved.

2. Coach helps to define or reconfirm measures of success for what the client wants to accomplish in the session.
3. Coach explores what is important or meaningful to the client about what he or she wants to accomplish in the session.
4. Coach helps the client define what the client believes is needed to be addressed or resolved in order to achieve what the client wants to accomplish in the session.
5. Coach continues conversation in direction of client's desired outcome unless client indicates otherwise.

Competency 3: Creating Trust and Intimacy

1. Coach acknowledges and respects the client's work in the coaching process.
2. Coach expresses support for the client.
3. Coach encourages and allows the client to fully express him/herself.

Competency 4: Coaching Presence

1. Coach acts in response to both the whole person of the client and what the client wants to accomplish in the session.
2. Coach is observant, empathetic, and responsive.
3. Coach notices and explores energy shifts in the client.
4. Coach exhibits curiosity with the intent to learn more.
5. Coach partners with the client by supporting the client to choose what happens in the session.
6. Coach partners with the client by inviting the client to respond in any way to the coach's contributions and accepts the client's response.
7. Coach partners with the client by playing back the client's expressed possibilities for the client to choose from.
8. Coach partners with the client by encouraging the client to formulate his or her own learning.

Competency 5: Active Listening

1. Coach's questions and observations are customized by using what the coach has learned about who the client is and the client's situation.
2. Coach inquires about or explores the client's use of language.
3. Coach inquires about or explores the client's emotions.

4. Coach inquires about or explores the client's tone of voice, pace of speech or inflection as appropriate.
5. Coach inquires about or explores the client's behaviors.
6. Coach inquires about or explores how the client perceives his/her world.
7. Coach is quiet and gives client time to think.

Competency 6: Powerful Questioning

1. Coach asks questions about the client; his or her way of thinking, assumptions, beliefs, values, needs, wants, and so on.
2. Coach's questions help the client explore beyond current thinking to new or expanded ways of thinking about himself or herself.
3. Coach's questions help the client explore beyond current thinking to new or expanded ways of thinking about a situation.
4. Coach's questions help the client explore beyond current thinking towards the desired outcome.
5. Coach asks clear, direct, primarily open-ended questions, one at a time, at a pace that allows for thinking and reflection by the client.
6. Coach's questions use the client's language and elements of the client's learning style and frame of reference.
7. Coach's questions are not leading, that is, do not contain a conclusion or direction.

Competency 7: Direct Communication

1. Coach shares observations, intuitions, comments, thoughts, and feelings to serve the client's learning or forward movement.
2. Coach shares observations, intuitions, comments, thoughts, and feelings without any attachment to them being right.
3. Coach uses the client's language or language that reflects the client's way of speaking.
4. Coach's language is generally clear and concise.
5. The coach allows the client to do most of the talking.
6. Coach allows the client to complete speaking without interrupting unless there is a stated coaching purpose to do so.

Competency 8: Creating Awareness

1. Coach invites client to state and/or explore his or her learning in the session about a particular situation (the what).

2. Coach invites client to state and/or explore his or her learning in the session about himself or herself (the who).
3. Coach shares what he or she is noticing about the client and/or the client's situation, and seeks the client's input or exploration.
4. Coach invites client to consider how new learning from the coaching will be used.
5. Coach's questions, intuitions, and observations have the potential to create new learning for the client.

Competency 9, 10, and 11: Designing Actions, Planning and Goal Setting, and Managing Progress and Accountability

1. Coach invites or allows client to explore progress towards what is wanted to be accomplished in the session.
2. Coach assists the client to design what actions/thinking client will do after the session in order for the client to continue moving toward the client's desired outcomes.
3. Coach invites or allows client to consider his or her path forward, including as appropriate, support mechanisms, resources, and potential barriers.
4. Coach assists the client to design the best methods of accountability for himself or herself.
5. Coach partners with the client to close the session.
6. Coach notices and reflects client's progress.

About the Author

Dr. Boysen-Rotelli is a coach and professor with a varied industry and professional background that includes supply chain and logistics, talent management, recruitment and selection, and professional coaching. These roles have spanned a number of industries as well as both public and private organizations. She completed her coach training education at the University of Texas at Dallas in the executive, professional, and career coaching program and received her Master Coach Certification (MCC) from the International Coach Federation. Dr. Boysen-Rotelli has served as an elected member of the executive board of the Chicago Coach Federation. Her doctoral studies at Benedictine University in organization development included extensive research on coaching and talent management. She holds a Bachelor of Science in marketing from the University of Illinois, an MBA with a concentration in organization behavior from Northern Illinois University and a professional human resources certification from the Human Resources Certification Institute. Dr. Boysen-Rotelli has been teaching at the undergraduate and graduate level for over ten years and she is passionate about helping people to succeed, grow in their leadership capacity, and find fulfillment in their ideal careers.

An Introduction to Professional and Executive Coaching, page 119
Copyright © 2018 by Information Age Publishing
119

Made in the USA
Columbia, SC
13 March 2022

57619187R00074